Suzanne E. Wells, MS
Editor

Horticultural Therapy and the Older Adult Population

Pre-publication
REVIEWS,
COMMENTARIES,
EVALUATIONS . . .

"**T**his book is a must-read for anyone whose job is to facilitate successful aging. Here is a rich collection of articles on the research and application of people-plant interaction studies. . . Timely and well-written, this work takes a closer look at the role of horticulture in improving the well-being of older Americans. I believe this should be required reading for all professionals committed to a higher quality of life for seniors and geriatrics.

Horticultural Therapy and the Older Adult Population points to the potentials for expanding options in later life through horticulture. . . "

D0162190

Joel Flagler, MFS, HTR
Associate Professor
Agricultural Extension Agent
Rutgers University-Cook College

"**H**orticultural Therapy and the Older Adult Population is a compendium of ten articles written by eighteen international professionals, representing expertise in horticultural therapy, other therapies, gerontology, medicine and architecture. . . this is not an activity book *per se* (although some activities are described), but a programming book and it emphasizes planning and gaining administrative support prior to programming. The articles give you 'how-to' descriptions for using and incorporating horticulture as therapy, whether you are starting a program or integrating activities to meet patient goals into an existing program. Programs designed for Alzheimer patients, short and long term skilled nursing and co-treatment patients, aquired aphasia patients, and programs for intergenerational populations are highlighted. Discussions of stress reduction for care-givers and the sociocultural interactions found in older adult residences help round out the syllabus, addressing the needs of therapists. The facts that our society is steadily aging and that gardening is a dominant leisure adult activity, make this book a timely addition to our profession.

. . . The book concludes with an annotated description of programs across America and a thorough bibliography to help readers continue their studies. Practicing therapists and administrators can find support for developing programs using horticulture as therapy."

Douglas L. Airhart, PhD, HTM
Professor
School of Agriculture
Tennessee Technological University
Past President
American Horticultural Therapy Association

The Haworth Press, Inc.

Horticultural Therapy and the Older Adult Population

Horticultural Therapy and the Older Adult Population

Suzanne E. Wells, MS
Editor

with

American Horticultural Therapy Association
and *Friends Organization*

The Haworth Press, Inc.
New York • London

Horticultural Therapy and the Older Adult Population has also been published as *Activities, Adaptation & Aging*, Volume 22, Numbers (1/2)(3) 1997.

The development, preparation, and publication of this work has been undertaken with great care. However, the publisher, employees, editors, and agents of The Haworth Press and all imprints of The Haworth Press, Inc., including The Haworth Medical Press and Pharmaceutical Products Press, are not responsible for any errors contained herein or for consequences that may ensue from use of materials or information contained in this work. Opinions expressed by the author(s) are not necessarily those of The Haworth Press, Inc.

Cover design by Marylouise Doyle

The Haworth Press, Inc., 10 Alice Street, Binghamton, NY 13904-1580 USA

Library of Congress Cataloging-in-Publication Data

Horticultural therapy and the older adult population / Suzanne E. Wells, editor.
      p. cm.
    Includes bibliographical references and index.
    ISBN 0-7890-0036-9 (alk. paper).—ISBN 0-7890-0045-8 (pbk. : alk. paper)
    1. Occupational therapy for the aged. 2. Gardening–Therapeutic use. 3. Alzheimer's disease–Patients–Rehabilitation. 4. Aphasics–Rehabilitation. I. Wells, Suzanne E.
RC953.8.022H67 1997   97-6431
615.8′51′0846–dc21   CIP

INDEXING & ABSTRACTING

Contributions to this publication are selectively indexed or abstracted in print, electronic, online, or CD-ROM version(s) of the reference tools and information services listed below. This list is current as of the copyright date of this publication. See the end of this section for additional notes.

- ***Abstracts in Social Gerontology: Current Literature on Aging,*** National Council on the Aging, Library, 409 Third Street SW, 2nd Floor, Washington, DC 20024

- ***Abstracts of Research in Pastoral Care & Counseling,*** Loyola College, 7135 Minstrel Way, Suite 101, Columbia, MD 21045

- ***AgeInfo CD-ROM,*** Centre for Policy on Ageing, 25-31 Ironmonger Row, London EC1V 4QP, England

- ***AgeLine Database,*** American Association of Retired Persons, 601 E Street, NW, Washington, DC 20049

- ***Alzheimer's Disease Education & Referral Center (ADEAR),*** Combined Health Information Database (CHID), P.O. Box 8250, Silver Spring, MD 20907-8250

- ***Brown University Geriatric Research Application Digest "Abstracts Section,"*** Brown University, Center for Gerontology & Health Care Research, c/o Box G-B 235, Providence, RI 02912

- ***Cambridge Scientific Abstracts,*** *Risk Abstracts,* Environmental Routenet (accessed via INTERNET), 7200 Wisconsin Avenue #601, Bethesda, MD 20814

- ***CINAHL (Cumulative Index to Nursing & Allied Health Literature), in print, also on CD-ROM from CD PLUS, EBSCO, and SilverPlatter, and online from CDP Online (formerly BRS), Data-Star, and PaperChase. (Support materials include Subject Heading List, Database Search Guide, and instructional video).*** CINAHL Information Systems, P. O. Box 871/1509 Wilson Terrace, Glendale, CA 91209-0871

(continued)

- ***CNPIEC Reference Guide: Chinese National Directory of Foreign Periodicals,*** P.O. Box 88, Beijing, Peoples Republic of China

- ***Combined Health Information Database (CHID),*** National Institutes of Health, 3 Information Way, Bethesda, MD 20892-3580

- ***Communication Abstracts,*** Temple University, 303 Annenberg Hall, Philadelphia, PA 19122

- ***Family Studies Database (online and CD/ROM),*** National Information Services Corporation, 306 East Baltimore Pike, 2nd Floor, Media, PA 19063

- ***Health Care Literature Information Network/HECLINET,*** Technische Universitat Berlin/Dokumentation Krankenhauswesen, Sekr. A42, Strasse des 17. Juni 135, D 10623 Berlin, Germany

- ***Human Resources Abstracts (HRA),*** Sage Publications, Inc., 2455 Teller Road, Newbury Park, CA 91320

  IBZ International Bibliography of Periodical Literature, Zeller Verlag GmbH & Co., P.O.B. 1949, d-49009 Osnabruck, Germany

- ***INTERNET ACCESS (& additional networks) Bulletin Board for Libraries ("BUBL"), coverage of information resources on INTERNET, JANET, and other networks.***
  - JANET X.29: UK.AC.BATH.BUBL or 0006012101300
  - TELNET: BUBL.BATH.AC.UK or 138.38.32.45 login 'bubl'
  - Gopher: BUBL.BATH.AC.UK (138.32.32.45). Port 7070
  - World Wide Web: http: / / www.bubl.bath.ac.uk./BUBL/ home.html
  - NISSWAIS: telnetniss.ac. uk (for the NISS gateway)
  The Andersonian Library, Curran Building, 101 St. James Road, Glasgow G4 ONS, Scotland

- ***Leisure, Recreation and Tourism Abstracts, c/o CAB International/CAB ACCESS . . . available in print, diskettes updated weekly, and on INTERNET. Providing full bibliographic listings, author affiliation, augmented keyword searching,*** CAB International, P.O. Box 100, Wallingford Oxon OX10 8DE, United Kingdom

(continued)

- *Mental Health Abstracts (online through DIALOG),* IFI/Plenum Data Company, 3202 Kirkwood Highway, Wilmington, DE 19808

- *National Clearinghouse for Primary Care Information (NCPCI),* 8201 Greensboro Drive, Suite 600, McLean, VA 22102

- *New Literature on Old Age,* Centre for Policy on Ageing, 25-31 Ironmonger Row, London EC1V 3QP, England

- *OT BibSys,* American Occupational Therapy Foundation, P. O. Box 31220, Rockville, MD 20824-1220

- *Psychological Abstracts (PsycINFO),* American Psychological Association, P. O. Box 91600, Washington, DC 20090-1600

- *Referativnyi Zhurnal (Abstracts Journal of the Institute of Scientific Information of the Republic of Russia),* The Institute of Scientific Information, Baltijskaja ul., 14, Moscow A-219, Republic of Russia

- *Social Planning/Policy & Development Abstracts (SOPODA),* Sociological Abstracts, Inc., P. O. Box 22206, San Diego, CA 92192-0206

- *Social Work Abstracts,* National Association of Social Workers, 750 First Street NW, 8th Floor, Washington, DC 20002

- *Sociological Abstracts (SA),* Sociological Abstracts, Inc., P. O. Box 22206, San Diego, CA 92192-0206

- *Special Educational Needs Abstracts,* Carfax Information Systems, P. O. Box 25, Abingdon, Oxfordshire OX14 3UE, United Kingdom

- *Sport Database/Discus,* Sport Information Resource Center, 1600 James Naismith Drive, Suite 107, Gloucester, Ontario K1B 5N4, Canada

(continued)

SPECIAL BIBLIOGRAPHIC NOTES

related to special journal issues (separates)
and indexing/abstracting

☐ indexing/abstracting services in this list will also cover material in any "separate" that is co-published simultaneously with Haworth's special thematic journal issue or DocuSerial. Indexing/abstracting usually covers material at the article/chapter level.

☐ monographic co-editions are intended for either non-subscribers or libraries which intend to purchase a second copy for their circulating collections.

☐ monographic co-editions are reported to all jobbers/wholesalers/approval plans. The source journal is listed as the "series" to assist the prevention of duplicate purchasing in the same manner utilized for books-in-series.

☐ to facilitate user/access services all indexing/abstracting services are encouraged to utilize the co-indexing entry note indicated at the bottom of the first page of each article/chapter/contribution.

☐ this is intended to assist a library user of any reference tool (whether print, electronic, online, or CD-ROM) to locate the monographic version if the library has purchased this version but not a subscription to the source journal.

☐ individual articles/chapters in any Haworth publication are also available through the Haworth Document Delivery Services (HDDS).

ABOUT THE EDITOR

Suzanne E. Wells, MS, is Supervisory Environmental Scientist with the U.S. Enviromental Protection Agency. She is the past President of the board of Garden Resources of Washington, a nonprofit organization that helps people in The District of Columbia help themselves by growing food, beautifying neighborhoods, and becoming enviromental stewards. By developing and maintaining community gardens and green spaces, they are able to enhance the overall quality of life in their communities. Ms. Wells is a leadership member of the Friends of Horticultural Therapy organization, through which she supports horticultural therapy research, education, and information dissemination.

Horticultural Therapy and the Older Adult Population

CONTENTS

Introduction

Suzanne E. Wells

In 1981, the American Horticultural Therapy Association (AHTA) published "HortTherapy: A Comprehensive View of Horticulture and the Aging." Since this publication became outdated, the Friends of Horticultural Therapy (FOHT), an AHTA support organization, decided to support development of an updated publication.

FOHT was founded in 1988. Its purpose is to promote horticultural therapy by:

1. Providing public information about horticultural therapy and enabling gardening techniques;
2. Supporting research and education to advance the profession of horticultural therapy; and
3. Helping develop horticultural therapy programs through financial and technical assistance.

This publication, *Horticultural Therapy and the Older Adult Population,* is intended to provide more current information on the field. It is hoped this publication will stimulate networking and information sharing among the horticultural therapy and other professionals working with older adults, spur new ideas and foster continuing research.

In this volume, you will find articles on garden designs to enhance the horticultural therapy experiences of older adults, descriptions of existing horticultural therapy programs for older adults, and new research to evaluate the effectiveness of horticultural therapy with this population.

Also, in this collection, are the results of a survey sent to all registered members of AHTA who work with the older adult population. The survey responses cover general information about the institutions and the popula-

[Haworth co-indexing entry note]: "Introduction." Wells, Suzanne E. Co-published simultaneously in *Activities, Adaptation & Aging* (The Haworth Press, Inc.) Vol. 22, No. 1/2, 1997, pp. 1-2; and: *Horticultural Therapy and the Older Adult Population* (ed: Suzanne E. Wells) The Haworth Press, Inc., 1997, pp. 1-2. Single or multiple copies of this article are available for a fee from The Haworth Document Delivery Service [1-800-342-9678, 9:00 a.m. - 5:00 p.m. (EST). E-mail address: getinfo@haworth.com].

tion served, programming activities, program staffing, program evaluation, and funding.

Finally, the collection includes a bibliography prepared as a service to horticultural therapists and others working with older adults. While the bibliography is not exhaustive, it attempts to include the most relevant publications to persons involved with horticultural therapy programs or research on older adults.

Many people contributed their time and ideas to this special collection. I would like to thank the following: the authors of the papers for their willingness to share their ideas, and their responsiveness in preparing their papers; the peer reviewers for their insightful comments; Diane Relf of the Department of Horticulture at the Virginia Polytechnic Institute and State University for the extensive bibliography she graciously shared and Suzanne DeMuth from the University of Maryland, College Park, for the literature search she conducted; Steve and Diane Hubin for their assistance in compiling the results of the questionnaires in a database; Nancy Stevenson in her role as Chairperson of FOHT for conceiving this project; Steven Davis and Sharon Simson for their direction on the overall project; David Houseman for his willingness to review all the papers and provide significant comments regarding the overall structure of the special collection; The Haworth Press for its willingness to publish this special collection; and Joyce Potkay, who held the entire project together by her perseverance and good nature.

Finally, included in this special collection is a pull-out card with membership information on AHTA and FOHT. If you don't already belong to these organizations, please consider joining them.

The Paradise Garden:
A Model Garden Design
for Those with Alzheimer's Disease

Margarette E. Beckwith
Susan D. Gilster

SUMMARY. This paper investigates the design of garden spaces for individuals with Alzheimer's disease. The paradise garden is used as a model for a restorative environment. This model for people with Alzheimer's Disease can be a resource for designers, healthcare providers and others interested in places which contribute to well-being. One of the key issues addressed is that of memory and the gradual decline experienced by those affected with Alzheimer's. Current and recent research provide a basis for integrating certain landscape elements into the garden design. Historical precedents further confirm the preference for similar elements. The components of the paradise garden are analyzed as they apply to the abilities of the population under consideration. Finally, the paradise garden model provides a basis for the design of three gardens at a specialized Alzheimer's facility in southwest Ohio. Each garden addresses the unique environmental, social and physical needs for each population along the continuum of Alzheimer's disease. *[Article copies available for a fee from The Haworth Document Delivery Service: 1-800-342-9678. E-mail address: getinfo@haworth.com]*

Margarette E. Beckwith, ASLA, is Principal and Owner of Beckwith Chapman Associates, Architects and Landscape Architects, P.O. Box 246, Oxford, OH 45056.

Susan D. Gilster, RN, BGS, NHA, is Executive Director of the Alois Alzheimer Center, 70 Damon Road, Cincinnati, OH 45218.

[Haworth co-indexing entry note]: "The Paradise Garden: A Model Garden Design for Those with Alzheimer's Disease." Beckwith, Margarette E. and Susan D. Gilster Co-published simultaneously in *Activities, Adaptation & Aging* (The Haworth Press, Inc.) Vol. 22, No. 1/2, 1997, pp. 3-16; and: *Horticultural Therapy and the Older Adult Population* (ed: Suzanne E. Wells) The Haworth Press, Inc., 1997, pp. 3-16. Single or multiple copies of this article are available for a fee from The Haworth Document Delivery Service [1-800-342-9678, 9:00 a.m. - 5:00 p.m. (EST). E-mail address: getinfo@haworth.com].

3

The paradise garden, as myth, metaphor and tradition, provides a model for designing outdoor spaces for individuals with Alzheimer's disease. The designer can focus upon aspects of design issues that may be less important to the unaffected group of individuals, but are critical to the Alzheimer's population. These aspects deal with "memory." First, there is *personal* memory, the repository of information amassed from earliest recollections, expanded daily and hourly as our lives unfold. Next, there is *genetic* memory, or those survival-based, innate responses (Kellert & Wilson, 1993). Finally, there is *archetypal memory*, those deep cultural images lodged in our consciousness. This paper takes the position that two means of confirming the effectiveness of a proposed exterior space and associated elements are revealed in current and recent research into the response to the natural setting and historic precedents which have seeped into our psyches through cultural traditions. Based upon the review of these bodies of information, an application of the concepts is presented in the form of three gardens designed for a specialized Alzheimer's facility in Cincinnati, Ohio.

WHAT IS ALZHEIMER'S DISEASE?

Alzheimer's disease is a progressive, irreversible brain disease that affects approximately four million Americans today. Although first described in 1907 by Dr. Alois Alzheimer, there is no known prevention or cure. Generally beginning in the later years of life, the disease is initially noticed through subtle changes in a person's ability to remember things. As the disease progresses, additional cognitive functions are affected, such as language, abstract thinking and physical functions, eventually leaving an individual dependent on others for all their care and daily needs. In the early stages of the disease, cognitive abilities and memory are not significantly impaired. The individual has relatively unchanged capacities for perceiving the environment and for remembering objects and space. The short-term memory is the first casualty of this disease. This decline takes with it the day-to-day, hour-to-hour recall of events. The names and identities of those most recently known and other more current experiences are often not remembered. For many, the ability to move, to walk and to be physically active remains. Wandering, determined walking or moving in a less directed mode is also a characteristic of the disease. This activity seems to relieve stress, as walking does for any unafflicted person, and it provides healthful exercise. However, due to diminished cognitive capacity, the individual frequently gets lost causing anxiety for individuals as well as the caretakers.

As the disease progresses, reducing the individual's short-term memory, the individual's long-term memory becomes the designer's resource. Images, or things that played a part in earlier years or childhood, remain in varying degrees as a connection to the past, providing memories and pleasures from an earlier phase of one's existence.

The continued decline of the cognitive abilities poses further challenges to the participant. In time, the disease leaves the individual unable to walk independently. The person's capacities seem to be confined to the pleasures of the moment within an ever confining arena. Exactly how much and which sensory abilities continue to function is not known at this time. But one could surmise that some very basic responses to the environment still exist. These are the innate responses, those bonded to our genetic heritage. Beyond the senses of touch, smell and sight, lie the innate preferences. It is at this stage that the job of the designer to enrich the environment is most critical, maximizing the quality of life. Facilitating independence and maximizing capabilities through environment and therapeutic programs, aids in enhancing life's pleasures and creating joy. This is important because in most cases, death occurs many years after the earliest signs of the disease and subsequent diagnosed symptoms.

SELECTED CURRENT RESEARCH

The natural environment is an effective way of assisting individuals and families during the intervening months or years. It is in the relationship to nature that deepest memory seems to be most closely bonded. Current research and empirical evidence of the beneficial effects of nature are extensive, giving credence to the concept of biophilia. The study of preferences and affinity to plants, animals and life processes has resulted in a wealth of valuable information for the designer. The *Biophilia Hypothesis,* a book assembled by Kellert and Wilson (1993), is an eloquent series of essays, hypothesizing upon the origins of these pleasures. It is Wilson's theory that response to the natural environment is genetically based. The affinity an individual has to a setting, he states, is strongly determined by survival instincts established "thousands or millions of years ago" (Wilson, 1993). This survival tactic became the experience influencing the genetic memory bank. One facet of this affinity has been studied for many years by Rachel Kaplan, an environmental psychologist. She has identified and described the mental activity involved in our interest in the natural environment. Kaplan defines "fascination" as "an absorbing, restful and rejuvenating state of mental alertness not derived from other settings" (Kaplan & Kaplan, 1989). This condition aids in the recovery from stress (Ulrich, 1991). More rapid recovery occurs when viewing natural scenes.

Recorded brain electrical activity data suggest that people were more wakefully relaxed during exposure to the natural landscapes (Ulrich, 1993).

Another topic of interest, particularly to the designer, is the response to the configuration and elements within the site. Ulrich and others have determined from many preference studies that there is a significant affinity to "savanna or park-like settings, including visual openness and uniform ground cover associated with large-diameter mature trees" (Ulrich, 1993). Distant, unobstructed views would most certainly have provided opportunities to see potential danger and escape. Heerwagen and Orians (1993), on the other hand, have identified other aspects of site which are of interest. They indicate there are major differences in the way groups of individuals respond to landscapes. Females, children, the elderly, as well as those who are physically ill or depressed, they deduce, should exhibit "a greater affinity to enclosures and protected places . . . "(Heerwagen & Orians, 1993). Women, possibly pregnant or with children, older people and those who are ill would be less successful surviving in the open. A place of shelter would offer a degree of security and refuge.

This evidence on the benefit of nature, and specifically the preferences for enclosed space and vistas, coupled with historical precedents, is the foundation for the direction taken in this project. It suggests the hypothesis that gardens, especially enclosed spaces, provide an environment preferred by certain groups of individuals (Heerwagen & Orians, 1993). This would include those with Alzheimer's disease.

HISTORICAL PRECEDENTS

Historically, the preference for gardens is chronicled in literature, in the pictorial arts and in the remains of buildings and garden spaces. The repeated creation of these spaces, in fact and record, indicate a preference for such environments as pleasurable space, as restorative space or as space needed or desired to complement life. An early example of the pleasure derived from gardens is exquisitely described in tomb paintings of ancient Egypt (600 B.C.E.). These describe ordered, productive and pleasurable enclosed spaces. Fruit trees, flowers, pools and fowl are painted with a degree of life and acuity that conveys a sense of understanding and fascination with the environment.

The text of *Gilgamesh*, a Sumerian document, offers one of the very earliest written descriptions of a restorative garden setting. Emerging from the region described as the "cradle of civilization" between the Tigris and Euphrates Rivers of the Middle East, this magnificent epic describes the reign of King Gilgamesh. This reign is thought to have occurred about 2700 B.C.E. (Kluger, 1992). Originally conveyed orally, it is recorded on a clay tablet in cuneiform. One segment describes a garden of restorative qualities. Although translations of the text vary, the essence is: "A garden of luscious fruit, of imperishable beauty and of whose inhabitants knew neither sickness, violence or aging" (Monyihan 1979), and " . . . a garden of precious stones, like an earthly paradise" (Gardner and Maier, 1984). This early culture in the Middle East placed high value on gardens, associating them with well being and everlasting beauty.

The paradise garden evolved from the same cultural roots as the Gilgamesh epic in the Middle East. A human-built oasis, the paradise garden was characterized by an enclosing wall, creating a space stocked with animals and planted with trees and plants of all kinds. Continuing as a garden tradition from earliest recorded time, it spread rapidly with events of the eighth century. On the wave of Islamic religious fervor, the paradise garden tradition moved across North Africa and the Straits of Gibraltar to Spain. Extending eastward, the influence of this landscape tradition seeped into the Mogul gardens of India and Kashmir. The garden setting of the Taj Mahal is probably one of the most well-known of the examples of this tradition. Having filtered into the Judeo-Christian tradition, images of the garden emerge in the Torah and the Old Testament. It seems to have penetrated into our cultural consciousness, becoming an archetypal image.

ELEMENTS OF THE GARDEN

In order to more specifically describe and analyze the model of the paradise garden as myth and as cultural phenomenon, it is worth considering the elements Moynihan (1979) identifies as being key. They are the: *enclosing wall, water, canopy and hill*. These four elements, along with the additional element of paving, provide a theoretical structure within which one can create a restorative space to meet the needs of the person with Alzheimer's disease.

Enclosing Wall

The enclosing wall creates the paradise garden. The term *"paradise"* is a transliteration of the Persian word *Pairidaeza: pairi-*, meaning around and *-daeza* meaning wall (Webster's, 1981). These enclosing walls associated with a residence, originally constructed of mud or stone, provided a degree of privacy essential to family life. The walls sheltered plants from the searing wind which swept the desert; they protected against undesirable entry of thief and wild beast; and they secured the space for pleasure of shade, fruit and flower. The sacred cedar, date palm, pomegranate, fig and grape vines can be identified from illustrations, and were among those plants nurtured here in a human-built oasis of pleasure and plenty.

For the individual with Alzheimer's disease, the walled or fenced space serves as a refuge. Judith Heerwagen and Gordon Orians (1993) conducted intriguing studies which reveal the desire for refuges. Spatial enclosures, they theorize, tend to be appealing to the elderly and those who are physically and psychologically vulnerable. These refuges, in contrast to the savanna or open space (Ulrich, 1993), provide a reduced level of danger. For the individual with Alzheimer's, there is similar appeal. Though they are not dealing with predators in the normal sense, they find the secured environment similarly effective. It provides a safe and secure space for exercise, walking and wandering, gardening and socializing. It allows contact with nature, while at the same time defining the limits of the space. It provides privacy, and offers a degree of dignity appropriate to these individuals. Whether this is a screen wall to prohibit the views of the public or picket fences the delineation of space is the basis of the paradise garden (Hoover, 1994).

Rachel Kaplan makes a strong case for the therapeutic benefit of accessible nature. Her compelling studies into the benefit of "nearby nature" can easily be achieved by incorporation of enclosed space (Kaplan and Kaplan, 1989). This component of the paradise garden makes the garden accessible to the individual with Alzheimer's disease.

The enclosed space, if planned correctly, can offer views from interior spaces or "places of refuge." The courtyard can provide changing views with the variations of daylight, night lighting, season and climatic conditions. These reminders are important for all, but particularly useful to those with diminished memory capacity. The aesthetic and affective experience of viewing the exterior space from within can be pleasurable, drawing attention to the natural environment. Whether it is the delicate lavender shadows of a summer evening, the snow-ladened landscape or the gentle swaying of foliage in the breeze, the effect of nature's display can be engaging, a source of comfort and peace. In the final analysis the enclosure, as was the case in the early desert situation, provides privacy, security and safety. It offers the opportunity for accessibility to exercise areas, to nature and to social contact.

Water

Water is a key feature in the paradise garden. One of the very early depictions of water being the source of all life is found in an ivory plaque from Assur, circa 1247-1207 B.C.E. This image describes a mountain, trees and a four-part river symbolizing the four rivers of life (Moynihan 1979). As an archetypal image, the concept seeps through history, appearing in Judeo-Christian religion. "And the Lord planted a garden eastward in Eden; . . . And out of the ground made the Lord to grow every tree that is pleasant to the sight and good for food; the tree of life also in the midst of the garden . . . and a river went out of Eden to water the garden and from thence it was parted and became four heads" (Bible, Genesis 2: 8-10). The motif was manipulated and refined by the early designers of the paradise gardens, examples of which are the courtyards of Isfahan and Alhambra. The same concept was interpreted by the Christian monks in designing the cloister garths.

Throughout history, water in garden design has been an important feature. Invariably, it has been located in a prominent location within the garden and considered a precious commodity. For both children and adults water holds an attraction rarely superseded by any other feature. Ervin Zube and others have conducted numerous studies which reveal the high preference for bodies of water, especially with a calm surface (Zube, 1978). Numerous researchers hypothesize this may be based upon humans' biological need for water. Whether or not the affinity for a water feature in the landscape is a genetically based preference, it is effective in its positive connotation (Ulrich, 1993).

For individuals with Alzheimer's disease, water can be experienced on a number of different levels. From a more cognitive perspective, when the symptoms are mild, it can be seen symbolically. The aesthetic appeal of an attractive fountain can be extremely effective in a garden. Hearing the gentle murmur of a stream of water is also soothing. As the cognitive abilities diminish, the response can be one of a more affective or pre-cognitive nature. Illicited from the deeper memory, the aesthetic response, suggested by some to be genetically based, remains. Beyond these visual reactions is the physical. Dipping a hand into the cool liquid can be another means of sensory stimulation.

Canopy (Tree or Trellis)

The canopy is another powerful delineation of limit–the ceiling. As Heerwagen and Orians (1993) hypothesize, the tree plays an important role in human survival. It offers the potential for food, refuge, shade and a vantage point for surveying the landscape (Bourliere, 1963; Isaac, 1983; Shipman, 1986, cited in Heerwagen and Orians, 1993). Formed by trees or trellis for shade, the canopy is as effective for the desert as it is for the temperate zone of North America. It can define a space; it shelters one from the intense sun; and it filters light to create a more gentle effect. This can be particularly satisfying when used at the entry of a building to create a transition between a relatively dark space to bright sunlight. This aspect is particularly important to older individuals whose eyes may be sensitive to glare.

Trees can be clues to climatic conditions. Tousled by the wind, the foliage flutters, sways or snaps, animating the space and providing an indication of the wind force. This can be a source of interest to the viewer.

Trees frequently indicate the existence of water or an oasis, offering not only the potential for water, but also the possibility of food. Historic examples are seen in Egyptian tomb paintings of Ammonhotep dating back to 1300 B.C.E. Here date palms and other fruit laden trees are depicted defining the parameter of the garden, while a trellis defines the center space. Grapevines, heavy with fruit, cover the frame creating an edible and decorative ceiling. One can only imagine the pleasure of that space of dappled light, luminescent foliage and fruit.

Another example of the trellis is illustrated in the alabaster relief of Assurbanipal of Nineveh, Assyria, 660 B.C.E. Here again the trellis of grapevines creates the ceiling, defining the space for pleasure. Alternating cedar and date trees provide the boundary of the space. Symbolizing the essence of royal pleasure, the king and a woman who is probably his wife, sip wine while being fanned and serenaded in this most pleasant setting.

Mount or Hill

The promontory, or hill, in the garden is represented in the paradise myth and in many cultures (Moynihan, 1979). The ancient ziggurat (a stepped building, a ladder to heaven) of Mesopotamia is one of the earliest large human-built structures, providing a sacred setting in an elevated situation. Other examples are the great Stupa at Sanchi (a sacred mound) and the burial mounds of the American Indians in southwest Ohio. The hill need not always be large to be effective. One need only see Japanese gardens, such as Ryoan-ji, where from within a sea of white gravel, emerge the realistic mountains. These Asian gardens were frequently designed as a visual experience.

In gardens for the Alzheimer's population, the hill is also a visual element. In this setting the "hill" must be subtle and, only a slight change in grade. Located in proximity to a seating area, the hill becomes a metaphor for the place of refuge, a place to allow vicarious wandering. It defines, by its alternative configuration, the flat zones in the garden.

Paving

Finally, the use of paving is another aspect of the Middle Eastern precedent readily applicable to our situation. Necessary in a situation of limited area and of high traffic volume, hard surfaces were used extensively in the Middle East. Addressing a similar situation, the garden for people with Alzheimer's disease is best served with selected zones of paved surfaces. To accommodate the use of walkers and wheel chairs, sufficient space should be provided. The problem of glare, particularly for older individuals, should be considered in the selection of paving material. A fine textured, slip resistant surface is essential. At the same time, the aesthetics of paving is a major factor in the space. Color, texture and the refinement of details all contribute to the affective response of the space.

THE MODEL APPLIED

The essential elements of the paradise garden—wall, water, canopy and mound—have been thematic components of the design of three therapeutic gardens at the Alois Alzheimer Center.

The Alois Alzheimer Center opened on May 1, 1987, in Cincinnati, Ohio, as a specialized facility dedicated exclusively to the care of individual's with Alzheimer's disease and dementia. The home, which accommodates 82 residents, provides a continuum of care. Evolving to meet the needs of its users, the facility is internally organized into three zones. Given the unique environmental, social and physical needs of each population along the continuum, one garden would not work. Therefore, an accessible garden space was designed for each group.

THE COURTYARD

The first garden to be constructed was the "Courtyard" (see Figure 1). This space is not unlike the early Middle Eastern precedent in that it became a focus for many of the adjacent interior rooms. The building, originally an elementary school, was adapted for use as an Alzheimer's facility. This single-level structure was designed in the era when bringing daylight into the classroom and allowing a child to view the landscape was considered an advantage. Generous windows face into the courtyard offering a "psychic" escape in summer, winter, day or night. Providing this visual access was one of the therapeutic goals established for the project. Another was the need for the loop path, a circuit walk. This would accommodate the "wanderers" and the walkers on a sinuous path of leisurely progression, offering a variety of views along the way. As a means of consistent reassurance, it delivers the user back to the origin of the journey. A well-defined path, avoiding the confusion and resulting disorientation of "dead ends," is found to be the most successful configuration. Benches are located at intervals, offering an opportunity to sit with visitors or rest and view the garden.

It is not necessary for all elements in the space to be participatory. The hill, or mount, as seen in the paradise garden or other ancient models, can provide visual interest and variety in the otherwise two dimensional ground plane. They give change, contour and mystery to the garden.

The generous patio is screened overhead by a trellis for both shade and psychological containment. It is a ceiling creating a degree of refuge. Nearby a small pool with a raised planter gives a focus to the space. The single jet of water gently ripples the pool surface, providing a quiet, comforting murmur.

A curved planted hedge designed to gently embrace the space is not high enough to obscure the view to the building entrance. It suggests enclosure of the sitting area. Raised planters facilitate the individual's desire to reach the soil, to plant a tomato or to smell the flowers. Elements that provoke memory can be included in many creative ways. Personal memories are stimulated by old fashioned plants: pansy, peony, snapdragon and nasturtium. Lavender, thyme and mint merge visual and olfactory pleasures. Tastes and fragrances tug effectively at the memory as Marcel Proust confirms, integrating into the situation what has been called "remembrance therapy" (Hoover, 1994). As recent memory declines, the remembrance of earlier times can become the source of pleasure. Finally, avoiding any plants with toxic attributes is an obvious choice.

THE SOUTH TERRACE

The second garden, the "South Terrace," is smaller–a contraction consistent with the abilities of the participant. The individuals using this space have lost a great deal of cognitive ability, but remain very active, continuing to "wander," sometimes with greater intensity than before. Disorientation is more pronounced, however. Here, a path needs to be more limited.

FIGURE 1. Courtyard Design

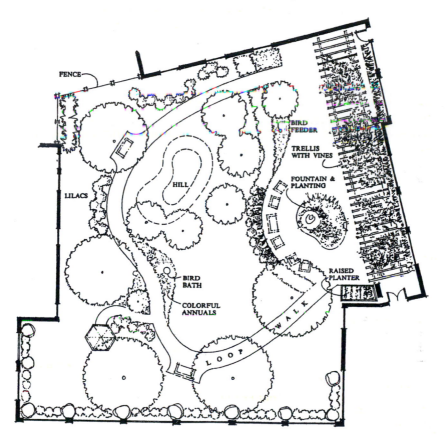

A planted island in the terrace provides a zone to be circumnavigated. The paving follows the gentle curve of a raised planter. Luxurious and colorful plants fill the planter. A small pool with fountain again acts as a focal point, drawing attention from the screen wall and fence which secure the space. Clusters of solid garden furniture are arranged beneath the trellis. The sunshine is stencilled through the fine covered trellis, in an ever-moving pattern on the paving below. Again, consistent with the concept of "nearby nature," the space must be fully accessible to ambulatory or non-ambulatory users.

THE WEST GARDEN

The "West Garden" area contracts the space still further for those further along the disease process. Need for a "wandering" loop gives way to an area configured to accommodate wheelchairs and comfortable, sturdy garden furniture. The canopy, once more a trellis, offers relief from the glare of the sun. The pool and fountain activate the space in a planter about 30 inches high. At this stage of the disease one of the remaining pleasures is tactile sensation. Plants are selected to provide that experience. Lamb's ear, dusty miller and ornamental grasses are all within reach–soft, velvety, rough and smooth. Color and fragrance are offered through an array of annuals, perennials and herbs. Again, reviewing all plant material as to potential toxicity is imperative. The cool water of a fountain offers a complementary experience.

CONCLUSION

The Courtyard was the first of the three gardens under construction. Installation of paving in mid-summer 1995 initiated the project. People love watching people and the construction drew a great deal of attention from the residents. Workers and heavy equipment, moving soil, defining the curbed planter, pouring concrete and seeding the aggregate–all these events drew absorbed curiosity and conversation from behind the glass. With the paving set up and the site cleared, the courtyard was reopened in its partially completed state.

People like the opportunity to be outdoors. Even before the planting was installed, the new path beckoned. Used by some as an exercise circuit, the more athletic individuals make their way around the loop in concerted strides. Others move at a more sedate pace, pausing to look and observe the surroundings from different angles or sit on one of the benches. Some residents avoid the path altogether or walk on and off as the inclination moves them. The generous paved area invites wheelchair users to the space. With the new paving of fine textured exposed aggregate, accessibility is facilitated. Walkers and wheelchairs move smoothly into the outdoor room.

Spring will see the trellis constructed and the vines installed to cover it. In the late summer red-orange flower trumpets will offer color and clumps of fine leaflets will screen the south exposure. It will create a ceiling to this exterior space.

The warmer months will allow a greater opportunity to study the use of the garden. Because the space was planted in late September, there was minimal time to observe the residents' response to the plant materials. A cold snap struck, terminating much of garden activity for the season. Fountain grass, pinks, forget-me-nots and fragrant lavender were installed. The deep yellow Stella d'Oro daylilies, enthusiastic and predictable bloomers that they are, were still flowering as they were set into the soil along the building and edge of the planting bed. Their presence was all-too-great a temptation for one enthusiastic resident. She began picking the flowers minutes after they were installed. Our hope that a few might remain for the opening of the new addition the following day came second to the satisfaction experienced by observing this avid gatherer pursuing a past pleasure. There is no greater confirmation of success than the pleasure in the face of this gardener, with her bright blue barrette, white hair and eager expression, as she loaded her arms with the yellow blossoms. The event christened the space; flowers are for the picking, for the smelling, for the touching.

As the construction process continues, the vortex of interest stimulated by the project draws in the curious family, friends, caregivers, students and all who intuitively sense the potential benefit of gardens. Just as the objective of life is the journey, so the therapeutic effect of the healing garden is the involvement of the participant, family, caregiver and perhaps even its designer. Although the search for a model began in the paradise garden, the key to these restorative spaces for people with Alzheimer's is providing the opportunity to return to where we began–in the garden. The description of a healing place which existed approximately 5000 years ago reminds us that our preferences as deduced by researchers and a review of historical precedents are probably correct. Nature is the continuum that offers a restorative relationship. When all else is in turmoil, particularly for individuals with Alzheimer's disease and their spouses and families, the garden offers peace, tranquility and quiet fascination. It provides a balm to the pain of grief; it gives comfort and security. It offers an opportunity to heal the spirit and, most important, it confirms our place in the universe of things.

REFERENCES

Gardner, John and Maier, John. (1984). *Gilgamesh* (translated from the sin-leqi-unninni version). New York: Vintage Press.

Heerwagen, J.H. & Orians, G.H. (1993). Humans, habitats, and aesthetics. In S.R. Kellert & E.O. Wilson (Eds.), *The Biophilia Hypothesis* (pp. 138-172). Washington DC: Island Press.

Hoover, Robert C. (1995). Healing gardens and Alzheimer's disease. *The American Journal of Alzheimer's Disease.* March/April.

Kaplan, R. and Kaplan, S. (1989). *The Experience of Nature.* A Psychological Perspective. Cambridge: Cambridge University Press.

Kellert, S.R. and E. O. Wilson. (Eds.). (1993). *The Biophilia Hypothesis.* Washington DC: Island Press.

Kluger, R. S. (1991). *The Archtypal Significance of Gilgamesh.* A *Modern Ancient Hero.* Einsiedeln, Switzerland: Daimon Verlag.

Merriam-Webster's Third New International Dictionary of the English language unabridged. (1981). Chicago: Merriam-Webster.

Moynihan, E. B. (1979). *Paradise as a Garden in Persia and Mughal India.* New York: George Braziller.

Ulrich, R.S., (1990). Aesthetic and affective response to natural environment. In I. Altman & J.F. Wohlwill (Eds.), *Human Behavior and the Environment: Vol. 6* (pp. 85-125). New York: Plenum.

Ulrich, R.S. et al. (1991). Stress recovery during exposure to natural and urban environments. *Journal of Environmental Psychology.* II, 201-230.

Zube, E.H., D.G. Pitt, and T.W. Anderson. (1975). Perception and prediction of scenic resources values of the Northeast. In E.H. Zube, R.O. Brush and J.G. Fabos (Eds.), *Landscape Assessment: Values, Perceptions and Resources.* (pp. 151-167) Stroudsburg, Pennsylvania: Dowden, Hutchinson & Ross.

Residential Landscapes:
Their Contribution to the Quality
of Older People's Lives

Jane Stoneham
Roy Jones

SUMMARY. Although it is well acknowledged that plants and gardens are often a source of great enjoyment to older people, little is known about how older people want to use the outdoors or about their preferences for different types of landscape. Current work at the Research Institute for the Care of the Elderly, UK, is looking at how well the grounds of purpose-built retirement housing are meeting the needs and preferences of residents. Questionnaire data, collected from approximately 100 sheltered housing residents, provide insights into the following issues: Importance of the grounds in retirement housing; use of the grounds and how this differs from what people did in their previous homes; values attached by residents to

---

Jane Stoneham, BSc (Hons) Horticulture MIEEM, MIoH, is Researcher and Landscape Consultant, Author of *Landscape Design for Elderly and Disabled People,* and Chair of the Federation to Promote Horticulture for Disabled People, UK. Address correspondence to: is 4 Green Cottages, Tyning Road, Combe Down, Bath BA2 5HG, UK.

Roy Jones, BSc, FRCP, FFPM, DipPharmMed, is Physician and Medical Gerontologist, and Director of The Research Institute for the Care of the Elderly. Address correspondence to: RICE, St. Martin's Hospital, Bath BA2 5RP, UK.

The authors would like to thank the Charities Aid Foundation for supporting this research through the Geoffrey Metcalf Legacy.

[Haworth co-indexing entry note]: "Residential Landscapes: Their Contribution to the Quality of Older People's Lives." Stoneham, Jane and Roy Jones. Co-published simultaneously in *Activities, Adaptation & Aging* (The Haworth Press, Inc.) Vol. 22, No. 1/2, 1997, pp. 17-26; and: *Horticultural Therapy and the Older Adult Population* (ed: Suzanne E. Wells) The Haworth Press, Inc., 1997, pp. 17-26. Single or multiple copies of this article are available for a fee from The Haworth Document Delivery Service [1-800-342-9678, 9:00 a.m. - 5:00 p.m. (EST). E-mail address: getinfo@haworth.com].

the landscape; interest in wildlife; and reasons why older people no longer garden. *[Article copies available for a fee from The Haworth Document Delivery Service: 1-800-342-9678. E-mail address: getinfo@ haworth.com]*

The subjective well-being of older people has been a focus for a wide range of research work which has covered many different aspects of the lifecourse (Larson, 1978). A number of researchers have highlighted the desire of most people to continue to live independently in retirement and the importance of the home environment to older people (Townsend, 1957; Gurney & Means, 1993). However, the attitudes of older people to the outdoor component of the home and the potential benefits that can be gained by appropriate design and management remain largely unexplored.

The idea that well-being can be enhanced by contact with the outdoor environment is well established in popular consciousness, but only in recent years has it received formal research interest (Relf, 1992). Much of this interest focuses on general responses to the natural landscape (Kaplan & Kaplan, 1989), but little of this work considers the potential influence of age. Although there are some notable studies in the field (for example, Burgess, 1990; Grahn & Berggren-Barring, 1995; Regnier & Pynoos, 1987; Talbot & Kaplan, 1991), there is still an important need to investigate the attitudes and preferences of older people toward the natural environment and the potential benefits that can be gained from promoting appropriate outdoor activity.

There is some evidence, largely anecdotal, that older people respond differently than do other members of society to environmental change and characteristics (Rohde & Kendle, 1994). For example, it is suggested that older people generally prefer more formal, controlled and horticulturally-traditional landscapes, but that younger age groups prefer more natural, wilder styles (Hitchmough, 1994).

For the past 10 years the Research Institute for the Care of the Elderly (RICE) and allied universities have collaborated on a series of research studies looking at the importance of the outdoor environment toward the well-being of older people. Recent research at RICE has explored older people's attitudes toward, and use of, gardens and grounds to examine more formally the preferences of older people.

The work initially focused on sheltered housing. Sheltered housing in the UK is accommodation for older people designed to enable residents to retain their independence within a supportive environment. Residents are frequently provided with a landscape selected for them by the management organization, and hence may not express their own preferences. Management may be more concerned with the overall appearance of the grounds than with allowing residents individual choice in their activities

(Stoneham & Thoday, 1994). It is also the case that even in settings where the architecture is designed with care, the landscape may present an unnecessary institutional image that suppresses individual expression (Stoneham, unpublished).

METHODS

The study was carried out in two parts: Semi-structured interviews were carried out in a sheltered housing complex and then a questionnaire, based on the results of the interviews, was distributed to the residents of five more sheltered housing schemes.

Semi-Structured Interviews

A sheltered housing complex was selected that contained three different types of facilities: those for frail elderly people (with communal dining facilities); those for more independent residents (with communal day room only); and those for the most independent residents (with no communal facilities). It was particularly suitable because the grounds contained a range of different styles including formal flower beds, low maintenance ground cover plantings and an informal wildlife area.

The complex is supervised on a daily basis by a number of managers who agreed to the interviewer attending coffee mornings and writing to all residents (47 total) asking if they would be prepared to take part. All residents were subsequently asked if they would agree to be interviewed. Twenty-nine residents, (19 women and 10 men), took part in the interviews. The 18 non-participants included nine people who were excluded for reasons of ill health or inability to communicate, five people who did not want to take part, three people in the hospital and one recently bereaved person.

The residents interviewed were from the following age groups: 60-74, 32%; 75-84, 56%; 85-94, 12%. All had lived in the sheltered housing for at least 1 year. (The longest period of residency was seven years, since the opening of the complex.) The interviews explored a wide range of issues including: residents' life histories in relation to interest in plants and gardening; use of gardens prior to moving to sheltered housing; problems associated with gardening; use of present sheltered housing landscape; values attached to the landscape; importance of views from indoors; interest in wildlife; and the social role of gardens.

The interviews yielded useful, detailed information about the perceived importance of the landscape to the elderly residents, the ways in which the outdoors is used and some of the factors which dissuade people from using it more. These findings were used to develop a more focused questionnaire for distribution to the wider sample in the second part of the study.

Questionnaire

The questionnaire was structured so residents could complete it themselves. Five sheltered housing schemes, widely accepted as having high quality landscapes, and with a total of 196 residents, were selected. Completed questionnaires were collected from 106 residents (84 women and 22 men). The participants were from the following age groups: 60-74, 34%; 75-84, 46%; 85-94, 20%. Most (93%) had lived in sheltered housing for at least one year; the maximum time any participant had lived in sheltered housing was 12 years. Over 50% had lived in sheltered housing for less than five years and, of those, nearly half had lived there for less than two years.

ANALYSIS

Because of the similarity in the information requested, the data from the questionnaire and the interview were combined, except for the section considering the values attached to the grounds which was only included as part of the questionnaire. Data were statistically analyzed using the chi-square (χ^2) test to see:

1. If there was a significant difference in the use of the sheltered housing grounds in comparison with the use of the grounds in residents' own homes.
2. If there was a significant difference in the values attached to the grounds of sheltered housing by women in comparison with men.

In the case of small numbers, the Yates Correction factor was applied.

FINDINGS

Use of the Grounds

Residents were asked whether they performed various activities in sheltered housing "often," "occasionally" or "never." The main relevant findings are shown in Figure 1.

FIGURE 1. Use of the grounds in sheltered housing

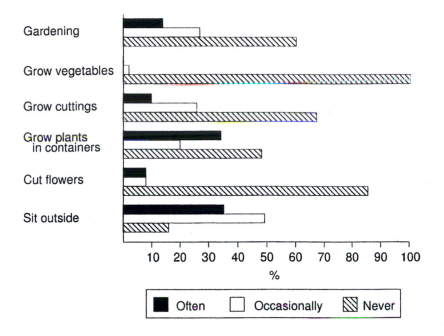

The main use of sheltered housing landscapes appeared to be passive: Most people said they sat outside when the weather was good either "often" or "occasionally." Active use was less common. The interviews also revealed the importance of relationships and social contact with other residents and staff in influencing people's attitudes toward, and use of, the outdoors. For example, in one housing scheme there is an active gardening club from which non-member residents feel excluded.

The residents were asked whether they had performed various activities in their previous homes "often," "occasionally" or "never." Ninety-four percent of the subjects had lived most of their lives with a garden prior to moving to the sheltered housing. Figure 2 shows the main relevant activities carried out in their previous homes.

It is of particular interest to see the extent to which the activity profile changed following the move to sheltered housing. A strong theme which emerged was the significant reduction in range and frequency of residents' outdoor activities in sheltered housing compared with their previous homes. All activities shown in the graphs declined in a highly statistically

FIGURE 2. Use of the grounds in previous homes

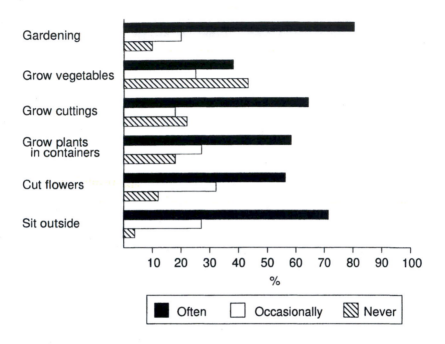

significant way (probability < 0.01). Most people used the gardens and grounds less frequently and for a narrower range of functions than they did those of their previous homes. One activity (growing vegetables) stopped completely and all others declined in frequency. For all activities, the numbers of residents responding that they "never participated" were greater in sheltered housing compared with their previous homes.

Although these figures may reflect changes which accompany aging and which may be motivating factors for the move to sheltered housing, they also raise important questions about people's opportunities, expectations and aspects of self-identity when they decide to move to retirement accommodations.

The decision of an older person to move to sheltered housing usually indicates a self-perception of aging and the need for some degree of support. Of those respondents who gave reasons for no longer gardening, "poor health" or "too old" featured highly. The former is arguably easier to quantify in terms of how health can limit people's abilities and ease of doing different things, but people's own perception of their age and what this means is harder to identify. Society imposes strong age-related pressures concerning appropriate behavior and lifestyles. It may also be the case that behavioral norms within the sheltered housing community suppressed some activities; indeed, it emerged from the interviews that some activities being abandoned were not beyond the apparent physical abilities of the residents. Thus, an important area of future study would be to clarify which activities reflect changing perceptions and revised expectations, and could therefore be maintained by inputs from outside, as opposed to those which reflect genuine difficulties.

Importance of the Grounds of Sheltered Housing

A fundamental question in the study was whether residents of sheltered housing considered the landscape to be important. The results showed overwhelmingly that the grounds were considered important; in fact, all but one of the respondents valued them.

Interestingly, this concern for the grounds was felt even by people who were not happy with the way the landscape had been designed (14% of the sample) or was being managed (7%). Approximately 15% of the people questioned were not making obvious use of the grounds, and yet still regarded the landscape as important to them. This finding emphasizes how misleading it can be to evaluate a landscape by using simple criteria such as satisfaction with particular aspects (e.g., style, layout and management) or by focusing on active use (e.g., by observing how often people sit outside). Passive uses and values, such as image, pride, conversation topics or views, can be expected to take on especially great importance in an elderly population growing increasingly frail (Jones, 1989).

Values Attached to the Grounds

Another important aim of the research was to identify values and meanings which older people attach to the outdoor environment. The self-completed questionnaire included a list of values suggested through the results of the personal interviews which also corresponded to the environmental values raised in other studies (Rohde & Kendle, 1994).

Residents were asked the question, "If you have a garden now, or if you use the grounds, do you see the outdoors as . . . (pick as many as you like)." Figure 3 lists the 20 options, and shows the percentage of respondents, identified by gender, who identified with the suggested values.

It is interesting to note that over two thirds of the respondents said that the landscape was "important for the image of their home." This was the largest single response to any of the values listed; this was especially obvious in the men's responses.

FIGURE 3. Values attached to the grounds of sheltered housing

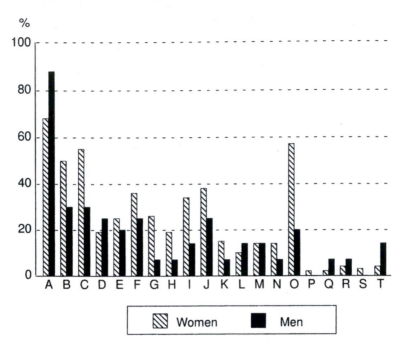

A: ". . . important for the image of your home"
B: ". . . a topic of conversation"
C: ". . . a place to socialise"
D: ". . . a place for solitude"
E: ". . . a place to be yourself"
F: ". . . beneficial to your overall health"
G: ". . . a means to relieve stress"
H: ". . . a means of keeping fit"
I: ". . . something to keep you active"
J: ". . . a means of having contact with wildlife"

K: ". . . captivating or absorbing"
L: ". . . stimulating and exciting"
M: ". . . fun"
N: ". . . a place to be creative"
O: ". . . providing things to look forward to"
P: ". . . productive"
Q: ". . . more useful for other members of the family"
R: ". . . a chore or duty"
S: ". . . a worry"
T: ". . . an expense"

    Approximately half of the women and a one quarter of the men said the grounds were important as "a topic of conversation," "a place to social-ize" and because they provide "something to look forward to." Other aspects that rated moderately highly, but with less clear gender difference, were a "contact with wildlife" and "benefits to overall health." About one third of the women considered the grounds to be "a means to relieve stress," "a means of keeping fit" or something that "helps them to keep active." The response of the men to these issues was less marked.

The only values which scored higher with men than with women were: Gardens are important to "image," and for "solitude"; gardens were more useful for other members of the family"; "gardens were a chore and an expense." These observations must be interpreted cautiously since in no case was there a statistically significant difference between males and females. Establishing significance was inevitably more difficult because there were fewer men in the study. Nevertheless, there may be a tendency for men, as compared with women, to underrate the positive personal potential of grounds.

Overall, it is encouraging that few of the respondents saw the grounds as an "expense," a "chore" or a "source of worry." This is true despite the fact that in sheltered housing, residents pay a clearly identified service charge to cover maintenance costs.

CONCLUSIONS

Sheltered housing was originally developed to enable older people to live independently within a supported environment. The design and management of the buildings, and to a lesser extent the grounds, place particular emphasis on making tasks easier or eliminating tasks altogether. Generally, less attention has been given to more intangible aspects relating to the quality of an older person's home life and the importance of continued activity.

The use of grounds and gardens is rarely seen as a necessity, despite its potential for encouraging mental and physical activity or fostering social contacts. This study shows that the outdoor environment is valued by residents even though they may not actively use it. The dramatic change in activity profiles associated with moving to sheltered housing highlights the fact that, even if technical barriers to access are removed, there may be powerful attitudinal and behavioral constraints. While social cliques within the sheltered housing and peer pressure may sometimes be responsible, more important are management regimes that favor easy maintenance over individual choice (Stoneham & Thoday, 1994).

To realize the potential benefits of gardening and contact with nature in old age, there must be a change in attitude. Patterns of land allocation and site design must be reconsidered to emphasize domestic style and provision of private territory. A key issue will be a change in management thinking; because more user-friendly solutions are not necessarily more expensive. It is important to create an atmosphere in which residents feel involved and able to influence their environment. To quote Rudyard Kipling, "The glory of the garden lies in more than meets the eye."

REFERENCES

Burgess, C.W. (1990). Horticulture and its application to the institutionalized elderly. *Activities, Adaption & Aging, 14(3)*, 51-61.

Grahn, P. & Berggren-Barring (1995). Experiencing parks. *Ecological Aspects of Green Areas in Urban Environments, 5.97*. XVIIth IFPRA World Congress, Antwerp.

Gurney, C. & Means, R. (1993). The meaning of home in later life. In S. Arber & M. Evandrou (Eds.), *Aging, Independence and the Life Course*, pp. 119-131 London: Jessica Kingsley.

Hitchmough, J. (1994). *Urban Landscape Management*. Sydney: Inkata Press.

Jones, R.W. (1989). Being old–A geriatrician's viewpoint. In J.A. Stoneham & A.D. Kendle (Eds.), *Therapeutic Horticulture for Disabled and Elderly People*, pp. 3-4. Gillingham, UK: Federation to Promote Horticulture for Disabled People.

Kaplan, R. & Kaplan, S. (1989). *The Experience of Nature; A Psychological Perspective*. New York: Cambridge University Press.

Larson, R. (1978). Thirty years of research on the subjective well-being of older Americans. *Journal of Gerontology, 33*, 109-125.

Regnier, V. & Pynoos, J. (1987*). Housing the Aged: Design Directives and Policy Considerations*. New York: Elsevier.

Relf, D. (Ed.). (1992). *The Role of Horticulture in Human Well-Being and Social Development*. Oregon: Timber Press.

Rohde, C.L.E. and Kendle, A.D. (1994*). Human Well-Being, Natural Landscapes and Wildlife In Urban Areas*. Peterborough: English Nature.

Stoneham, J.A. (1995). The living environment: Its effects on the wellbeing of older people. Unpublished Research Report. Bath: The Research Institute for the Care of the Elderly.

Stoneham, J.A. & Thoday, P.R. (1994*). Landscape Design for Elderly and Disabled People*. Woodbridge: Antique Collector's Club.

Talbot, J.F. & Kaplan, R. (1991). The benefits of nearby nature for elderly apartment residents. *International Journal of Aging and Human Development, 33(2)*, 119-130.

Townsend, P. (1957). *The Family Life of Old People*. Harmondsworth: Penguin.

Innovations in Intergenerational Programs for Persons Who Are Elderly: The Role of Horticultural Therapy in a Multidisciplinary Approach

Georgia Abbott
Virginia Cochran
Alicia Ann Clair

SUMMARY. Most intergenerational programs combine young children with elderly persons, but the benefits of intergenerational programming can be extended to include people of other ages. This article describes an innovative model program at the Colmery-O'Neil Veterans Affairs Medical Center in Topeka, KS, incorporating patients who are middle-aged with those who are elderly in multidisciplinary, therapeutic applications designed to facilitate treatment objectives for all. This article articulates the conceptual framework for integrating these patients, who range in age from 35 to 100 plus

Georgia Abbott, BS, HTR, is Director of Internship Training, Colmery-O'Neil Veterans Affairs Medical Center.

Virginia Cochran, MEd, CTRS, is Director of Therapeutic Recreation Services, Colmery-O'Neil Veterans Affairs Medical Center, Nursing home care unit.

Alicia Ann Clair, PhD, RMT-BC is Professor, Director of Music Therapy and Associate Faculty Member in Gerontology at the University of Kansas, Lawrence. She is also Research Associate at the Colmery-O'Neil Veterans Affairs Medical Center.

Address correspondence to: Colmery-O'Neil Veterans Affairs Medical Center, 2200 Gage Boulevard, Topeka, KS 66622.

[Haworth co-indexing entry note]: "Innovations in Intergenerational Programs for Persons Who Are Elderly: The Role of Horticultural Therapy in a Multidisciplinary Approach." Abbott, Georgia, Virginia Cochran, and Alicia Ann Clair. Co-published simultaneously in *Activities, Adaptation & Aging* (The Haworth Press, Inc.) Vol. 22, No. 1/2, 1997, pp. 27-37; and: *Horticultural Therapy and the Older Adult Population* (ed: Suzanne E. Wells) The Haworth Press, Inc., 1997, pp. 27-37. Single or multiple copies of this article are available for a fee from The Haworth Document Delivery Service [1-800-342-9678, 9:00 a.m. - 5:00 p.m. (EST). E-mail address: getinfo@haworth.com].

years, into horticultural and recreational therapy interventions. Therapeutic goals for all patients include sensory stimulation; social interaction and integration; feelings that they are essential members of a group; engagements with others in relationships; opportunities for self-esteem and self-worth; and positive, enjoyable experiences. *[Article copies available for a fee from The Haworth Document Delivery Service: 1-800-342-9678. E-mail address: getinfo@haworth.com]*

A search of the literature reveals that intergenerational programming refers to the incorporation of two very different client populations participating together in programs which function to meet the needs of all persons involved (Bocian & Newman, 1989). Most often these two populations include children of varying ages and persons who are elderly. Though no information described the incorporation of persons who are middle-aged with those who are elderly into intergenerational programs, the goals are compatible with those articulated for traditional intergenerational programs such as (a) Decreased isolation (Ventura-Merkel, Liederman, & Ossofsky; 1989); (b) Feelings of improved self-esteem and life satisfaction (Seefeldt, 1989); (c) Improved tolerance among the generations (Henkin & Sweeney, 1989); (d) Increased physical and mental well-being (Perspectives in Health Promotion and Aging, 1995); and (e) A sense of purpose (Perspectives in Health Promotion and Aging, 1995). In meeting these goals, it is essential to define clearly the objectives of the program, incorporate well-trained staff, have support from administrators, provide sensitively for the expectations of program participants, collaborate with appropriate service providers, recognize volunteers and professional participants, maintain appropriate leadership, confine the program to a manageable size and conduct ongoing evaluations (Ventura-Merkel et al., 1989).

PROGRAM PURPOSE

The purpose of the intergenerational model program at the medical center is the mutual benefit of all patients regardless of age and disability. Program applications are designed to meet individualized objectives for patients in a broad age range while providing the opportunities for social integration. Younger, middle-aged patients assist the physically frail older nursing home care patients and develop a sense of feeling needed while they contribute to the well-being of others. Patients who are elderly receive the younger patients with unconditional acceptance, and indicate clearly their enjoyment through shared camaraderie. Because all patients are veterans, they have a mutual respect for one another's contributions to country. They share in their feelings of patriotism and loyalty, and in their values of freedom, dignity and justice.

Though these veterans share feelings and values, they have disabilities which impede their opportunities to interact appropriately and meaningfully with one another without intervention. The younger patients have symptoms associated with post traumatic stress disorder, depression, substance abuse and psychiatric disorders. Older patients are generally physically frail and may have dementia, depression and other conditions associated with aging.

These patients, no matter what their ages or diagnoses, share in their needs for sensory stimulation; social interaction and integration; feelings that they are essential members of a group; engagement with others in relationships; opportunities for self-esteem and self-worth; and positive, enjoyable experiences. Treatment goals are designed to meet these common needs while allowing for individual differences in degree of need. For instance, patients with high need for self-esteem can help other patients who have high need for physical assistance. As these patients interact with one another, and positive responses occur, the patients who facilitate them are gratified. Consequently, gratification through successful experiences leads to a sense of accomplishment tied closely to feelings of self-esteem for those who provided the assistance and for those able to experience success because of it. Mutual benefits for all patients therefore occur as they experience success and enjoyment together. To assure such positive outcomes, these experiences are structured by interventions designed and implemented by trained professionals.

The purpose of this article, therefore, is to articulate the conceptual framework for designing and implementing a multidisciplinary, therapeutic program, incorporating horticultural and recreational therapies, to benefit persons of middle and old age. This information can then be used, in whole or part, to enhance programming in other settings for other persons in this age range.

PROGRAM CONCEPTS

Patients with varying needs differ in their physical abilities, their emotional responses and their social skills. These patients also have varying capacities for responsibility, whether it is in regard to accountability for their own behavior or it is related to their sensitivity and compassion for others. Therapeutic programs must, therefore, provide opportunities for successful experiences regardless of the individual skill levels of those involved.

The program at the Colmery-O'Neil Veterans Affairs Medical Center in Topeka, KS, described here incorporates individual skills with expectations for achievement at the level most suitable for each individual patient. Therapeutic applications are designed to include a broad range of response levels, and it is the integration of patients of different ages into them that facilitates individual achievements. Most of these activities have a number of components with time durations appropriate for the completion of required tasks. Those patients with large capacities for cognitive focus and physical endurance are required to maintain their involvement for longer periods of time than are physically frail patients who may also experience cognitive declines due to dementia or other illnesses.

Program Development

Program development requires careful planning and evaluation to ensure success. Consequently, plans must include all facets of the program and evaluation must be integrated into all phases of the plan to determine program effectiveness. The bottom line question must be answered: Did the activity, event, or project meet treatment objectives, and therefore benefit, individual patients?

To answer this question in the Veterans Affairs Medical Center, evaluation is conducted both formally in written reports included in individual patients' charts and informally within the context of patients' verbal discussions. Whether formal or informal, evaluations are made in consideration of each individual patient's treatment/care plan, and with regard to patients' responses, both verbal and participatory. Evaluation is therefore built into each session and includes: Observations of patients' engagement in particular activities including duration of participation and whether it is active or passive; patients' comments regarding enjoyment of the activity and assessment of the extent to which specific objectives for individual patients were met.

With evaluation procedures in place, therapeutic activities begin with careful staff planning. Collaborations between the horticultural therapist and the recreational therapist in the program described here function to design programs suitable for individual patient care plans. These programs constitute the processes through which behavioral outcomes are reached; and, while the processes are important, the best possible products are essential in order for patients to have satisfactory experiences. None of this can be accomplished, however, without the cooperation of nursing staff and others involved directly in patient care. Consequently, schedules for specific therapeutic application plans are cleared with nursing staff prior to implementation, and any assistance from nursing staff is approved in advance. Therapeutic activities for special events, such as picnics, 100th year birthday parties and holiday parties are scheduled as far as one year prior to the planned dates.

Preparation for a large scale event such as a holiday party or a theme party requires the contributions of individuals associated with many services in the medical center, including horticultural therapy, recreation therapy, music therapy, nursing, dietary, social work, medicine, pharmacy, psychology, engineering and housekeeping. In addition, family members and volunteers are asked to become involved at the level most comfortable for them.

Programs are more likely to be successful when all persons involved in them are requested to participate for the benefit of the patients. Contributions of assistance, materials or resources are solicited, and the only requirement is that any commitment that is made must be met.

Procedures for developing programming for such events include: (a) Meeting with the nurse manager to approve dates, (b) Selecting a theme with input from patients, staff, and family members; (c) Meeting with other therapists to secure their involvement, outline their tasks and define their responsibilities; (d) Ordering supplies and decorations; (e) Ordering food three or more weeks before the event, depending upon the amount and type; (f) Confirming responsibilities of all staff upon initial arrangements and again one week prior to the event; and (g) Confirming arrangements, room space, equipment reservations and all particular details when the initial planning is complete and again at least one week before the event. To assure task completion at specified times, follow-up memos defining individual tasks and their time lines are essential.

Program Implementation

One example of a very successful party event incorporated contributions and commitments from many persons. It occurred when the horticultural and recreational therapists requested staff, family, and volunteer involvement for a "Beach Party" in the nursing home care unit of the medical center. Both therapists worked with the nursing care residents and the middle-aged hospitalized patients to plan the event. The patients worked together for nine weeks to develop the party environment. With guidance from the therapists, a list of equipment and materials was made and the appropriate supplies were ordered.

As patients became involved in working together, the horticultural and recreation therapists requested participation from nursing staff, dietary service workers, music therapists, housekeeping staff, family members and volunteers. Patients and therapists sent invitations to individuals throughout the medical center, including the medical center director, the chief of staff and the physician in charge.

Horticultural and recreation therapists solicited input from patients concerning every component of the event. Patients suggested bringing sand and plants to the unit for the party. They made menu suggestions and requested live music. Dietary staff worked closely with the therapists to incorporate diet restrictions into the party food. One staff volunteered to make frozen, exotic, non-alcoholic drinks and worked with the therapists to submit a list of ingredients and equipment required, e.g., blenders, plastic glassware, paper umbrellas, special flavorings and juices.

The music therapy staff responded to the request for live music by asking patients and staff throughout the medical center who could play instruments or sing to participate together as a band. These musicians rehearsed for several weeks to develop the appropriate music repertoire and to perfect their ensemble. As a consequence of these rehearsals, additional patient treatment objectives were met. In fact, the experience was so rewarding that these persons continued to get together regularly to play music long after the party was over.

Family members and volunteers participated in developing the party materials. Some made party decorations or brought materials from home. Family members and volunteers came to the party to assist those needing help and to contribute to the festiveness of the occasion.

Patients who were physically able worked with the horticultural therapist to select tropical plants from the greenhouse, to groom the plants and to ready them for transport to the nursing home care unit. The horticultural therapist also worked with these patients to procure containers appropriate to use for miniature beaches. They located sand on the medical center grounds, requested and received permission to use it, and shoveled it into the containers stored at the greenhouse until the party.

Meanwhile, patients from nursing home care and other patients involved in the program worked with the horticultural and the recreation therapists to make centerpieces for the tables. In addition, they planned where to place and how to incorporate into the activities party favors such as leis, grass skirts and straw hats. They also planned the sequence of activities within the event which included introductions by the medical center director, announcements of appreciation, presentations of picnic food and exotic drinks, music and dancing, placing bare feet into the sand containers and clean up. An event evaluation session for all patients was also scheduled.

Due to the physical layout of the medical center and the distance from the greenhouse clinic to the nursing home care unit, the horticultural therapist arranged for a vehicle and worked with patients to transport plants and sand containers to the nursing home care unit the day of the party. Both the horticultural and the recreation therapists assisted patients in arranging the plants, sand containers and other materials according to the plan they developed together.

As the event unfolded, all patients participated, no matter what their level of capability. Those patients on the unit with severe physical limitations were also included. The enthusiastic participation of all patients, staff, family members and volunteers attested to the event's success.

Evaluation of the event was conducted in two phases. The first phase was integrated into the event and consisted of observations of individual patients. The second phase was a follow-up session in which verbal responses to open-ended questions were solicited.

Individual patients were observed during the event in order to assess whether they followed directions; made eye contact with the therapists; turned to watch party events; exhibited positive facial expressions; and clapped their hands or the side of their wheelchairs in applause at the conclusion of the program. These observations of participation indicated nonverbal engagement in the program and were interpreted as positive in the program evaluation. In addition to these nonverbal indicators, several spontaneous comments were noted, e.g., "I'm sure having a good time. You ladies give a real nice party. I feel like I'm on a desert island. My, my, my!"

The follow-up evaluation session, attended by patients and available staff, extended the positive experiences of the event as all who participated reminisced about the party. Patients of all ages were asked several open ended evaluation questions in order to avoid leading their responses. These questions included the following: What did you think of the plants? Did you notice the table centerpieces? Would you like to do something like this again? Would you be willing to participate in making plans for next month? Are you willing to help carry out the plans next time?

Responses to these questions indicated clearly that the patients very much enjoyed the event, and they made verbal commitments to continue their involvement in future programs. Nursing staff followed the patients' comments with a request to allow the plants to remain on the unit. When the horticultural therapist solicited comments from the middle aged patients concerning their interest in the continued care and grooming of the plants on the unit, these patients unanimously volunteered their cooperation. They decided to leave the plants for the patients' continued enjoyment and care involvement.

As the evaluation sessions came to a close, verbal comments, coupled with the observations of patient participation during the event, led to the conclusion that the event was highly successful. Horticultural and recreation therapists then asked patients to indicate verbally their interest in a range of activities which could be included in future program plans. Therapists noted which activities which were most preferred and which were less appealing.

Ideas for Programming

The participation of patients and staff with family members and volunteers can be generalized to an extensive number of events with varying themes. These may include a Fourth of July celebration complete with fireworks; a Mardi gras party; a casino afternoon; a 1950s picnic including a vintage car show and period clothes; a Valentine celebration with cards from area school children and volunteer organizations; and an egg hunt in the spring involving children from local day care centers.

For these theme parties, patients of all age ranges enjoy working together to make table arrangements, flower arrangements for individual rooms, dish gardens, wreaths, wall hangings and decorations suitable for the season or holiday. Integrated with these horticultural activities at holiday parties and seasonal celebrations are live music, visits from family members and trips into the community to acquire materials for projects.

When planning an event, ideas can come from seasonal or holiday themes, and time of year determines whether activities are held indoors or outdoors. Some activities can take place in both venues, e.g., seeds can be either sown directly into outdoor plant beds or planted in peat pots in the early spring and transplanted into a raised bed on the patio when the weather is warm. Both bedding plants intended for outdoor landscaping and flowering plants intended for cutting and arranging can be used.

Vegetable seeds like flowering plant seeds can be either directly sown or planted in peat pots and transplanted later. Both vegetables and flowers require pruning, watering, weeding, fertilizing and harvesting or cutting which are all done outside. The harvested vegetables can be eaten during a meal in the dining room while cut garden flowers decorate the tables.

Whether these or other program ideas are used, the tasks involved in any program or event must be suited to the physical, social and cognitive functioning levels of individual participants. Some older persons may participate by observing and making suggestions based on past gardening experiences, and others may participate by amending the soil, moving the soil into pots or planters, and cleaning the area, among other tasks.

Both indoor and outdoor projects can be completed in one session or in a series of sessions, depending on the complexity of the tasks and the time each requires. In addition to those already mentioned, these projects can include propagating plant cuttings, potting plants, planting dish gardens and terrariums, arranging silk, dried and fresh flowers, making centerpieces for dining room tables each month, caring for plants given to individual patients who cannot tend them themselves, and making corsages and boutonnieres for nurses and veterans on the unit to honor them for birthdays and patriotic holidays.

Project Format

Whatever the project, whether it is completed in one session or over a series of sessions, the following format offers a model of an approach structured to meet appropriate objectives.

Nature of Involvement	Time Line in Minutes
Persons in Middle Age	
1. Gather at the greenhouse to prepare session	30
A. Assemble supplies and equipment	
B. Horticultural therapist demonstrates model	
2. Transportation to nursing home care unit	10
3. Greet persons in nursing home care unit and the recreation therapist	10
4. Demonstrate model	05
5. Distribute tools and equipment	05
Persons in Middle Age Combined with Older Persons	
6. Engage in mutual participation with both therapists facilitating	20
7. Critique completed projects	10
A. Positive comments are solicited	
B. Individuals' work is applauded	
C. Enjoy	
Persons in Middle Age	
8. Transport nursing home care residents to day rooms	10

9. Meet with horticultural and recreation therapists
   to discuss session   10
   A. Review accomplishments
   B. Plan or confirm next session
   C. Serve refreshments
10. Transport back to the greenhouse   10
11. Return equipment and supplies   20
    A. Disassemble and put away returned products
    B. Prepare for recycling

The total participation time in this model for persons outside the nursing care unit is two hours and 40 minutes, while the total time for residents in nursing care is 30 minutes. This format allows participation suited to individual ability levels and interests, and has facilitated successful participation for the persons involved in it over the past four years.

CONCLUSION

This model program incorporates persons who are middle aged with those who are elderly and has proven its viability over the past four years. Evaluations of approaches and program content have led to the information presented here. Such evaluation indicates that the approaches used in the program are effective in providing beneficial experiences to those who participate and that it motivates for staff involvement in multidisciplinary teamwork. Incorporation of any or all of the therapeutic approaches used in this program into other facilities is encouraged. Further study is indicated to determine the additional effects of the program on patients and staff.

REFERENCES

Bocian, K. & Newman, S. (1989). Evaluation of intergenerational programs: Why and how? *Journal of Children in Contemporary Society, 20,* 147-163.

Cramer, D. (Ed.). (1995). Intergenerational activities: A positive force for health promotion. *Perspectives in health promotion and aging, Vol. 10, No.1,* (pp. 1, 3, 7).

Henkin, N. & Sweeney, S. (1989). Linking systems: A systems approach to intergenerational programming. *Journal of Children in Contemporary Society, 20*, 165-172.

Seefeldt, C. (1989). Intergenerational programs–impact on attitudes. *Journal of Children in Contemporary Society, 20*, 185-189.

Ventura-Merkel, C., Liederman, D., & Ossofsky, J. (1989). Exemplary intergenerational programs. *Journal of Children in Contemporary Society, 20*, 173-180.

Horticultural Therapy
in the Skilled Nursing Facility

Teresia M. Hazen

SUMMARY. A description of the skilled nursing facility (SNF) and the impacts and demands of managed care on therapies are included. The horticultural therapy contribution in rehabilitation therapies is outlined. Two case studies describe the patient base. Two SNF programs are departments in the hospital setting where horticultural therapy is delivered as a co-treatment with occupational therapy, physical therapy and speech and language pathology staff or by the horticultural therapist alone. A variety of horticultural therapy services are provided as part of recreation therapy programming. Indoor, year-round programming is outlined along with outdoor activities. Success oriented projects for the short stay rehabilitation patient are noted. The treatment session format provides a consistent structure to optimize rehabilitation progress. *[Article copies available for a fee from The Haworth Document Delivery Service: 1-800-342-9678. E-mail address: getinfo@haworth.com]*

Horticultural therapy makes a significant contribution in rehabilitation programming and patient achievement of performance goals in the Legacy Health System Skilled Nursing Facilities of Portland, Oregon. The horticultural setting enhances the healing process and contributes to overall quality of life for patients, visitors and staff. The horticultural therapy (HT) program also serves as a significant marketing tool in setting Legacy services apart from other skilled nursing facilities (SNF) in the region.

Teresia M. Hazen, MEd, HTR, QMHP, is Horticultural Therapist, Legacy Health System, 1015 NW 22nd Avenue, Portland, OR 97210.

[Haworth co-indexing entry note]: "Horticultural Therapy in the Skilled Nursing Facility." Hazen, Teresia M. Co-published simultaneously in *Activities, Adaptation & Aging* (The Haworth Press, Inc.) Vol. 22, No. 1/2, 1997, pp. 39-60; and: *Horticultural Therapy and the Older Adult Population* (ed: Suzanne E. Wells) The Haworth Press, Inc., 1997, pp. 39-60. Single or multiple copies of this article are available for a fee from The Haworth Document Delivery Service [1-800-342-9678, 9:00 a.m. - 5:00 p.m. (EST). E-mail address: getinfo@haworth.com].

This article outlines the horticultural therapy program in two SNF settings in which teamwork among all therapies and levels of administration is essential for success. Five years of learning, contribution and creating opportunities by all therapy staff, patients, families, administrators, volunteers and supporters are summarized. Year-round programming ideas are offered. Horticultural therapy can be integrated into a skilled nursing facility to increase patient achievement of performance goals through highly meaningful, motivating and functional horticulture activities.

THE SETTING

Legacy Health System is an Oregon not-for-profit health care system. Included in the network are four hospitals, a home health agency, a medical equipment company, a nursing home, primary care clinics, immediate care centers, occupational medical clinics and a variety of other health care services. Good Samaritan Hospital and Medical Center and the Emanuel Hospital and Health Center comprise Legacy Portland Hospitals. Approximately 1000 patient beds are maintained. These two sites offer subacute care in the skilled nursing facilities (SNF) with rehabilitation services, including horticultural therapy. Legacy Extended Care is the organization unit for the two SNFs.

Skilled nursing care patients are admitted at any time around the clock. They may be admitted from the physician's office, an emergency department or directly from a hospital. The admissions criteria for skilled nursing facilities established by Medicare are followed.

The units are appropriate settings for patients who continue to need medical care and/or rehabilitation after the acute hospital stay. Average length of stay is eight to 12 days. Length of stay in this hospital system has been dramatically reduced, as is true in hospital systems across the nation. The implications of managed care on skilled nursing facilities are immediate and pervasive. Patients are leaving acute care departments much earlier and are more acutely ill upon arrival in subacute care. The range of horticultural therapy activities assists in meeting the needs of these patients even at bedside. Managed care patients represent a major change and opportunity for the health care industry.

Subacute medical care addresses a wide variety of diagnoses, including post-surgical, intravenous therapy, complex wound care, diabetes management and teaching, orthopedics, stroke, spinal cord injury, multiple trauma, amputation, respiratory, cardiology, oncology, AIDS, renal and burn. Horticultural therapy services are provided to all appropriate patients. The average age of the participating senior is 71. Over the five-year history some of the program patients have been readmitted three and four times for horticultural therapy services.

A skilled nursing facility is available at each of the two downtown hospital sites. The 40-bed Bishop Morris Care Center SNF moved into Legacy Good Samaritan Hospital and Medical Center in the spring of 1996. Before this, Bishop Morris Care Center was located one block away and operated as a hospital department. The Legacy Emanuel Hospital SNF maintains 27 skilled beds and is located in a building approximately one block from the main hospital. Patients are transported via an underground tunnel to the SNF. The two hospitals are separated by approximately two miles and the Willamette River.

Staffing

The horticultural therapist in the Legacy Portland Hospitals rehabilitation services designed and implemented both SNF horticultural therapy programs and provides consultation to therapists in other programs serving seniors with short- and long-term disabilities. Volunteers are also involved in garden maintenance and assist with treatment groups and individual patient activities.

HORTICULTURAL THERAPY SERVICES

Horticultural therapy services include group treatment sessions, individual sessions, the outdoor therapeutic garden setting for treatment groups and independent restorative use, the indoor plant-table area and a small library of reading materials about gardening.

Treatment Groups

Referrals for HT treatment groups or individual services are made by nursing, occupational therapy, physical therapy, recreation therapy and speech and language pathology. Service is requested via the referral form used by all staff at the SNF sites. Social service staff also make referrals and often observe their patients in the group treatment session. The interdisciplinary treatment team determines/confirms services where appropriate in the care plan. Patients also seek out HT and self-refer.

Currently, the treatment group schedule is as follows:

Bishop Morris Care Center SNF
        2:00-3:00 Tuesday and Thursday
        10:30-11:30 Saturday

Emanuel Hospital SNF
    4:00-5:00 Tuesday
    6:15-7:15 Thursday
    1:00-2:15 Saturday

The horticultural therapist needs about one hour for session preparation and transportation of patients. Clean up, charting and planning requires another hour. Additional time is needed for shopping and gathering of supplies.

Group sessions of three to five patients are usually a co-treatment with occupational therapy, physical therapy or speech and language pathology. In Oregon, these three therapies are able to bill for third party reimbursement. The group treatment allows for more efficient use of therapist time because the therapist can schedule several patients and co-treat during the hour with horticultural therapy staff. Revenue generation is increased and patient goals are met and enhanced in a highly motivating social setting. Patients no longer receiving rehab therapies continue to be scheduled by HT and recreation therapy. The horticultural therapist usually conducts these groups alone.

Occupational therapy staff find a functional fit with the horticultural activities and opportunity for achievement of patient performance goals. Physical therapist participation includes ambulating of patients to the sink area where they follow the "Procedure for Pot Washing" and to the plant table/counter to mist or water plants. Some patients practice the use of a walker with basket by taking items to the trash, getting water and other needed supplies. Physical therapy staff and the horticultural therapist review short-term patient goals for the week and devise the treatment activity.

Speech and language therapy staff consult regularly and co-treat. Patient goals range from improved speech intelligibility, increased yes/no reliability, eye contact and initiation. When completing the initial HT patient assessment, the speech assessment is a key piece in the information gathering. It provides essential and detailed information regarding patient cognitive function.

The format used for treatment groups is included in Attachment 1. This routine becomes familiar and reinforces patient learning. The plant area at each skilled nursing facility site is located in a corner of the recreation/dining room. The area is unsecured, except for some locking cupboards. Two double four-foot fluorescent lights are located over a counter or table. Both areas have windows providing minimal light. The fluorescent lights are on timers. Individuals are attracted to this area during unstructured time for observation, discussion and plant care. Treatment groups meet around the dining table.

Mobility Group

At least once every week, co-treatment therapies are used with patients to increase mobility skills. After managing the elevators to the second floor, patients arrive at the Garden Room overlooking the patio garden. Weather permitting, patients proceed out to the garden for additional mobility work, sensory stimulation, cognitive retraining and work toward other treatment goals.

Major objectives for this activity include pathfinding, elevator use and orienting patients to the outdoor garden setting. Patients are encouraged to use the garden during unstructured time while alone and with peers or families.

Nature Crafts

Included weekly in the horticultural therapy group treatment are various nature crafts. For independent activity, these projects are set-up in the recreation room or patients often take a set-up to their room to work. The sample pressed flower place card (Attachment 2) has been made in all settings, including families and patients working together during unstructured time.

Plant Sales

Plant sales are scheduled weekly. Patients assist with setup and serve as cashiers and sales staff. The speech therapist often schedules patients to work the sale in order to assess money handling skills. Crafts, patient propagated plants and purchased wholesale greenhouse grown annuals and perennials are offered at the sales. Revenues fund the supplies needed for the program.

Nature Study

Video programs with discussion and, when available, hands-on materials are included at least once monthly in scheduled nature study activities. These programs are also provided for evening independent viewing and in-room leisure activity.

ATTACHMENT 1

GARDENING GROUP SESSION FOR SHORT STAY

One hour session   Date:

1. Browse catalogs and magazine while patients gather around the table.

2. Introduction---Names with structured response

3. Orientation

4. What's in Bloom?

5. Task-oriented project

    Clean-up routine

6. Current Events

7. Closing/review/looking ahead

8. Evaluation Notes:

Printed with permission from Legacy Health System.

One-to-One Program

Horticultural therapy programming also includes individual sessions when patients are unable to join the group. Sessions are designed to encourage out-of-room activity as soon as possible, to provide sensory and social stimulation for the patient with decreased endurance or mobility, and to assist in meeting the leisure needs of patients.

The Patio Gardens

The outdoor garden sites are approximately 9000 square feet each. A variety of containers and raised beds are used in group and individual treatments. Water is available for independent watering tasks. Occupational therapy, physical therapy, speech therapy and social service staff use the outdoor setting for both formal and informal patient treatments. Staff have access to watering equipment and engage patients in watering activity for a wide range of treatment goals.

ATTACHMENT 2

Skilled Nursing Facilities
Horticultural Therapy Patients
Legacy Portland Hospitals

*Who loves a garden
Finds within his soul
Life's whole.*
— *Louise Seymour Jones*

Printed with permission from Legacy Health System.

Community Outings

Recreation therapy staff design community outings to parks, public gardens, botanical gardens, garden centers and natural areas. Physical therapy and occupational therapy staff often co-treat during these outings.

Intergenerational Programs

Two to three times yearly, intergenerational programs are offered involving patients and local school and community center children. Series are scheduled for five consecutive weekly sessions of one hour. This intergenerational linking is beneficial for both children and patients. Hospital public relations staff also find this to be a highlight for their press releases. This activity reinforces Legacy Portland Hospital's goals for community collaboration (Attachment 3).

PATIENT FOLLOW-UP

Patients are encouraged to maintain connection with the horticultural therapy program by newsletter and monthly visiting/participation opportu-

ATTACHMENT 3

Announcing

GROWING TOGETHER

An Intergenerational
Gardening Class Series

Sponsored by

Legacy Emanuel Skilled Nursing Facility
and
Portland Parks and Recreation
Vernon Elementary School Students

4:00 - 5:00 p.m.
Tuesdays; May 9th, 16th, 23rd
June 6th, 13th

****
For further information contact
Teresia Hazen, HTR
LPH Horticultural Therapist
(503) 227-3791

nities. *The Adaptive Gardener,* a bi-monthly newsletter, is mailed to former patients who sign-up to receive it. Gardening hints for the upcoming two-month period, adaptive strategies and tools, energy conservation techniques and monthly visitation dates are presented. One Saturday each month, patients are invited to return for a visit. A program/project is presented; personal progress is reviewed; free seeds, cuttings and plants are distributed; and refreshments are served. Each of these returning gardeners serves as a public relations agent when they return to the community setting.

PROGRESS CHECKS AND EVALUATION

Staff members are always eager to discuss patient involvement in HT activities as well as their own personal experiences (Attachment 4). They participate in annual trainings' through the Staff Development office. The Horticultural Therapy Worksheet (Attachment 5) prepared by the Staff Development Specialist is based on a handout, "What is Horticultural Therapy?" and a five-minute video segment of a group treatment session.

Legacy staff have conducted two annual horticultural therapy training workshops. These events are designed to provide continued training for Legacy personnel and also an opportunity for staff to serve as a training resource for the Pacific Northwest region. Legacy staff collaborate with Portland Parks and Recreation, mental health agencies, local gardening and horticultural retailers and other community agencies in presenting these workshops (Attachment 6).

SPECIAL NEEDS OF THE SENIOR POPULATION

In designing and providing horticultural therapy interventions, the skilled nursing facility staff identified special issues and needs of seniors that can be addressed through the healing aspects of horticultural therapy services:

1. Horticultural therapy helps to increase functional skills to pre-hospital level while helping patients cope with common aspects of aging.
2. Horticultural therapy can help patients deal with loss and grief.
3. The group treatment setting and restorative benefit of the garden provide opportunities for seniors to engage in essential life review.
4. Horticultural therapy can help patients reassess skills and develop transferable skills. A patient may not have been a gardener, but is able to enjoy plants and flowers with just minimal effort and in-

volvement. Those with a history of involvement learn or relearn adaptive strategies for indoor and outdoor gardening. Education focuses on the transferable skills and meaning. Washing the table after the session is directly related to personal grooming and self care. Continual reinforcement of the benefits of cognitive stimulation through horticulture appeals to most of the seniors. Increasing strength and endurance is an issue of highest priority when seniors enter the SNF, as most want to return to their own private homes.

5. The group is a reminder of the importance of social support. Many seniors are isolated in the home. Extended isolation is often a contributing factor in the decline of health.

6. Horticultural therapy can provide a "meaningful activity" concept of rehabilitation. Getting well can take place outside of the hospital bed, doing things that bring pleasure. "Did you ever imagine that you would be transplanting houseplants at the hospital?" This remark always elicits smiles and chuckles. Patients express pleasure that they have plants to take home along with their hand lotion and wash basin!

CASE STUDIES

The following two case studies provide a description of seniors involved in skilled nursing facility horticultural therapy services.

Case Study #1

Client: JP
Diagnosis: Dyspnea, Insulin Dependent Diabetic, Congestive Health Failure and Vertebral Basilar Insufficiency.
Hospital stay: 1/10/95 to 1/13/95
SNF stay: 1/13/95 to 3/8/95
Age and sex: 83 Male
Presenting problem: Presented to emergency room 1/10/95 with weakness and shortness of breath after a history of about one week which started with nausea/vomiting. The physician believes patient may have had a gastrointestinal virus that became more complicated due to diabetes and overall frailty. Patient has a history of vertebral insufficiency which is the cause of gait/balance problems.
Physical: Cataracts in both eyes, decreased hearing, ambulates with walker, decreased sensation in extremities due to peripheral neuropathy, decreased balance, short of breath and left leg brace.

Cognitive: Alert, oriented, long-term memory appears good, some decreased short-term memory and decreased safety awareness.

Emotional: Pleasant, cooperative, highly motivated, generally cheerful/friendly, but periods of tearfulness.

Social: Outgoing, interactive. Lives alone at home with several hours of housekeeping/personal care assistance daily. Wife died several years ago.

Vocational history: Baker

Horticultural experience indoors: Some houseplants. High interest and extensive knowledge of orchids.

Horticultural experience outdoors: Rhododendron, camellia and rose collections. Belonged to Portland Rose Society and the American Rhododendron Society. Photography of flowers.

Short term goals by 2/15/95: Increase endurance to 45-60 minutes. Safely ambulate to gardening group three times weekly. Follow safety precautions at Consistent with Supervision Level 4 Rusk Group Activity Treatment Procedure.

HT services: Gardening groups three times weekly, nature crafts two times monthly, independent activity in plant/garden areas, mobility training in the garden setting, plant sales weekly and the horticulture library.

Initiated by patient: Caring for plants throughout the facility, placing plants in the office/reception area, care of raised planter at the facility front entrance, shared Jackson & Perkins rose catalog with various peers and staff, and advised staff in rose selection and rose care, causing several staff to order roses. JB signed-up to receive *The Adaptive Gardener* newsletter and attended one return visit session since discharge.

Discharge notes: Patient was discharged to home with registered nurse, occupational therapy, physical therapy services and 8 hours supervision daily. Twenty-four hour supervision was recommended.

Status upon discharge

Cognition/perception: Alert and oriented. Follows multiple step directions. Demonstrated some decreased safety awareness and decreased insight into deficits.

Physical: Numbness continues in right digits and hand occasionally. Endurance has improved to point that he may occasionally become short of breath with moderate activity. Demonstrates decreased standing balance and often does not self-correct.

Activities of daily living: Requires contact guard assist/standby assist with kitchen management and other higher activities of daily living tasks. Needs cues for safety and proper body mechanics. At discharge he alternates use of assistive devices: wheeled walker with basket, straight cane and no device. Physical therapy notes that he self-corrected balance on most occasions during the home visit prior to discharge.

Case Study #2

Client: VS

Diagnosis: Stroke with right hemiparesis

Hospital stay: 12/18/94 to 12/21/94

SNF stay: 12/21/94 to 2/14/95

Age and sex: 81 Female

Presenting problem: Presented to emergency room 12/18/94. Fell and crawled to phone in one hour. History of hypertension and congestive heart failure.

Physical: Vision adequate with glasses, hearing adequate, slurred speech with weak volume, propels wheel chair, right hemiparesis, decreased endurance, decreased sitting balance.

Cognitive: Alert, oriented, periods of decreased memory, able to follow one-step commands.

Emotional: Pleasant, cooperative, motivated, labile, periods of tearfulness due to husband's death two months ago.

Social: Outgoing, interactive. Enjoys being with others. Lives alone at home.

Vocational history: Clerk at Woolworth's

Horticultural experience indoors: Some houseplants.

Horticultural experience outdoors: Vegetable gardening, lawn care, bulbs–tulips and daffodils as favorites.

Short term goals by 1/15/95: Hold head erect and increase vocal volume during group. By 1/30/95: Maintain sitting balance for 15 minutes while performing task oriented activity. By 2/15/95: Attend three garden groups per week to increase endurance to one hour of activity and to meet social needs.

HT services: Gardening groups three times weekly, nature crafts two times monthly, independent activity in plant/garden areas, mobility training in the garden setting, plant sales weekly and horticulture library. Signed up to receive *The Adaptive Gardener* newsletter. In discharge conference with VS and daughter, it was agreed that VS would benefit from planting and managing two to three 20-inch plastic pots with herbs and flowers on the accessible patio of the adult foster home. Daughter will purchase and assist with set-up. VS also took several of her houseplants to manage.

Discharge Notes: VS was discharged to adult foster home with home health physical therapy for one week.

ATTACHMENT 4

PROTOCOL FOR HORTICULTURAL THERAPY ASSESSMENT

The Glass Garden Horticultural Therapy program has used a 5 point scale to evaluate patients in their treatment sessions. The evaluation tool is for use with physically disabled and developmentally disabled individuals. Other disciplines may be able to adapt parts of this evaluation tool to work with other population groups. The five points are defined as follows:

5.   Independent. The individual will be considered independent if he or she is able to perform the task without instruction, verbal cues or physical prompts or assists during completion of task. The patient is also considered independent if they can complete a task after an initial instruction of the task. This has been added because horticulture is fairly new to most patients.

4.   Consistent/ w/supervision. The individual will be considered able to complete task with supervision only if he or she can complete the task with 1 verbal cue or direction clarification.

3.   Minimum Assist. The individual will be considered able to complete the task with minimum assist if he or she requires a combination of any or one of the following: 2 verbal cues or direction clarifications, 1 physical prompt and/or 1 physical assist.

2.   Moderate Assist. The individual will be considered able to complete the task with moderate assist if he or she requires a combination of any or one of the following: 3 verbal cues or direction clarifications, 2 physical prompts and/or 2 physical assists.

1.   Maximum Assist. The individual will be considered able to complete the task with maximum assist if he or she requires a combination of any or one of the following: 4+ verbal cues or direction clarifications, 3+ physical prompts and/or 3+ physical assists.

N/A   Non-Applicable. The evaluation point will be considered N/A if the patient does not have the physical or cognitive ability to attempt that task, or if the evaluation point did not have an occasion to express itself during the course of his or her treatment sessions.

ATTACHMENT 4 (continued)

Legacy Extended Care
HORTICULTURAL THERAPY
GROUP ACTIVITY TREATMENT PROCEDURE

Attendance:

M ___ T ___ W ___ TH ___ F ___
1/2 1   1/2 1   1/2 1   1/2 1   1/2 1

M ___ T ___ W ___ TH ___ F ___
1/2 1   1/2 1   1/2 1   1/2 1   1/2 1

Name: _____ Age: _____
Chart No.: _____ Room: _____
Diagnosis: _____
Disability: _____
Physician: _____

KEY
5 – independent
4 – consistent/ w/supervision
3 – minimum assist
2 – moderate assist
1 – maximum assist
N/A – non-applicable

TREATMENT GOALS:

MOBILITY:	5	4	3	2	1	N/A
Comes independently to HT session						
Comes on time to HT session						
Able to maneuver within the greenhouse						

PHYSICAL/PERCEPTUAL ABILITIES						
Performs horticultural tasks: bilaterally						
left-handed						
right-handed						
Able to grasp/release tools during activity						
Able to manipulate tools						
Able to manipulate plant and non-plant materials						
Able to fill pot accurately						
Able to center cuttings in pot						
Able to place cuttings in dibble holes						
Able to place plant in upright position						
Able to place scissors in proper position for cutting						
Selects correct stem when cutting from multi-stem plant						
Able to space cuttings in whole pot						
Able to work with plant materials: in front						
above head						
to sides						
Able to water plants with: 1 lb. can filled						
2½ lb. can filled						
Able to water plants accurately						
Able to wash hands &/or nails in sink						
Endurance permits completion of horticultural tasks						
Able to work on specimen plants (over 6" pot)						
Able to complete horticultural tasks correctly						
Able to find all materials on table for task						
Able to control physical problems/pain during task						

WRITING ABILITY						
Writes own name on plant label						
Writes date on label						
Writes plant name on label						
Handwriting is legible						

SOCIAL INTERACTION	5	4	3	2	1	N/A
Hearing impairment limits socialization						
Foreign language limits socialization						
Aphasia limits socialization						
Initiates interaction w/therapist						
Interacts once approached						
Interacts with peers						
Interacts appropriately with others						
Fits easily into group						
Responds accurately/appropriately to questions						
Able to make self understood						
Able to discuss physical conditions realistically						

COGNITIVE ABILITY						
Follows verbal &/or written directions: 1 step						
2 step						
more						
Follows demonstrated directions: 1 step						
2 step						
more						
Able to remember task sequence between sessions						
Able to focus on task						
Able to maintain attention span for 1 hour session						
Able to shift from one task to another						
Able to control behavior to complete tasks accurately						
Follows safety precautions						
Understands basic horticultural concepts						
Understands purpose of HT treatment						
Able to adhere to time schedule						
Aware of seasons, weather, whereabouts						
Able to overcome problems encountered during tasks						

EMOTIONAL STATUS						
Is willing to try new activities						
Seeks assistance when appropriate						
Has confidence in horticultural tasks attempted						
Perseveres on difficult tasks						
Able to control emotional status during tasks						

AVOCATIONAL INTERESTS						
Selects own plant material for propagation						
Shows interest in learning cultural practices of plants						
Maintains own plants propagated during treatment						
Anticipates taking plants home						
Visits greenhouse on own time at least 3 x/week						

CURRENT FUNCTIONAL STATUS:

PROJECTED TREATMENT PLAN:

_____
Therapist

Form credited to
NEW YORK UNIVERSITY MEDICAL CENTER
The Rusk Institute of Rehabilitation Medicine

ATTACHMENT 5

 *Horticultural Therapy Worksheet*

1. List 4 activities that may be included in a horticultural therapy program.

2. List 3 physical benefits of horticultural therapy.

3. List 3 intellectual benefits of horticultural therapy.

4. List 3 social benefits of horticultural therapy

5. List 3 emotional/psychological benefits of horticultural therapy.

Watch the 5 minute video on a Horticultural therapy session here at Legacy. What was one of the benefits stated by one of the patients?

Name_____ Date_____

ATTACHMENT 6

LEGACY EXTENDED CARE

Presents

ADAPTATIONS FOR ACCESSIBILITY

**Horticultural Therapy and Gardening Activity with Emphasis on
Physical, Cognitive, Psychosocial and Sensory Adaptations**

**Thursday, July 20, 1995
7:30 A.M. to 5:00 P.M.**

**Lorenzen Conference Center
Legacy Emanuel Hospital
2801 N. Gantenbein
Portland, Oregon**

Sponsored by Legacy Health System

LEGACY
Health System

ADAPTATIONS FOR ACCESSIBILITY
Horticultural Therapy and Gardening Activity with Emphasis on Physical, Cognitive, Psychosocial and Sensory Adaptations

OBJECTIVES
* Acquaint participants with techniques for adapting gardening and horticultural activities for physical, cognitive, psychosocial, and sensory enhancement.

* Increase awareness of strategies to employ the natural setting year-round both indoors and outdoors for all ages, with special emphasis toward program development for rehabilitation, social, recreational and educational programming.

* Understand how to integrate gardening and horticultural activity, activity of high value and meaning in our society, into the rehabilitation model to increase client functional skills.

* Increase awareness of simple, low-cost techniques that can be easily replicated in your facility or program.

WHO WILL BENEFIT?
Healthcare, recreation, education professionals and volunteers who work in the following areas:

Activity Coordinators
Adult Foster Care Providers
Educators
Horticulturists
Medical Rehabilitation Therapists
Nursing Home Administrators
Social Workers
Recreation Program Staff
Vocational Rehab Counselors

REGISTRATION INFORMATION
The registration fee for this conference is $45. A salad bar lunch is an additional $5. The nature crafts class is project-oriented and requires advance registration and fee of $5.

CONTINUING EDUCATION UNITS
* Application has been made for .1 accreditation from the American Horticultural Therapy Association.
* Application has also been made for additional accreditation from the National Association of Social Workers, Oregon Parks and Recreation Association and Oregon Board of Examiners of Nursing Home Administrators.

Conference Schedule

Thursday, July 20, 1995

7:30   **Registration & Refreshments**
      Displays

8:00   **Hospital Tour**

8:45   **Welcome and Keynote Introduction**
      Stephani White
      Kevin Winslow
      Katie Kiely
      Teresia Hazen

9:00   **Realm of the Senses: Designing the Healing Garden**
      Research has addressed how interaction with nature, including horticultural therapy, can increase cognitive function, the ability to focus, and the tendency to seek out new experiences. But what is a healing environment, and how should it be designed? Mr. Epstein will present examples of healing gardens and explore the opportunities for therapists and landscape architects to collaborate in the design of rehabilitation gardens.

      Mark Epstein, ASLA
      Mitchel, Nelson, Welborn, Reiman Partnership
      Portland, Oregon

10:00   BREAK
      DISPLAYS

10:30   CONCURRENT SESSIONS - A

    1.   **Sensory Integration through Horticulture Activity**
        Shelby Atwood, OTR/L
        Horizons Day Program
        Garlington Community Mental Health Center

    2.   **Language, Communication and Cognition: Increasing Functional Skills through Horticultural Therapy**
        Pam Parker, SLP, MS,CCC

    3.   **Understanding the Americans with Disabilities Act**
        TBA

    4.   **Dialogue with Keynote Presenter**
        Mark Epstein, ASLA

    5.   **Creating a Marketing Niche**
        Exceed Customer Expectations by Providing Exceptional Horticulture and Gardening Programming
        Tom DeJardin

11:45   LUNCH

Informal Topic Groups over Lunch -
            SESSIONS - B

    1.   **Hand Skills and Horticulture**
        Marsha Josh, OTR/L

    2.   **Functional Mobility in Gardening Activity**
        Mary Eileen Barr, PT

    3.   **Container Gardening Strategies**
        Jerry Anderson, BS

    4.   **Horticulture Activity in the Adult Foster Care Setting**
        Erin LaRose, COTA/L

    5.   **Horticulture Activity and Children**
        Nita Oliver, MN

ATTACHMENT 6 (continued)

1:00   CONCURRENT SESSIONS - C

    1.   **Horticulture: Meaningful Activity and Psychosocial Benefits**
Susan Sherborne, MS, CTRS
Joan Meyerhoff, BSW
Legacy Extended Care

    2.   **Houseplant Identification, Characteristics and Special Uses in the Therapy Program**
Cheryl Straw
Portland Nursery

    3.   **Adopt-A-Garden: A Model for Hospital, Institutional, and Business Settings**
Involve staff and volunteers in teamwork for beautification
Jan Shea, LPH Community Relations
Dan Loper, LPH Material Services
Bonnie Rushing, LPH Volunteer Services

    4.   **Vocational Programming for the Developmentally Disabled: Adaptive Strategies and Special Tools**
David James, BS, Executive Director
Greenleaf, Grants Pass, Oregon
This session from 1:00 - 3:30

2:15   BREAK

2:30   CONCURRENT SESSIONS - D

    1.   **Basic Medical Terminology for Activity Providers**
Susan Sherborne, MS, CTRS

    2.   **Horticultural Therapy in the Skilled Nursing Facility: A Rehab Model with OT, PT, SLP Co-treatments**
Teresia Hazen, HTR
Eric LaRose, COTA/L

    3.   **Know Your Plants: Toxicity and Dermal Irritant Factors**
Oregon Poison Center Staff

    4.   **Adaptive Tools for Gardening**
Jerry Anderson, BS
Vocational Rehab Counselor
Zoraida Andreakos, AC
Mt. St. Joseph Residence

3:45   CONCURRENT SESSIONS - E

    1.   **Outdoor Plant Identification Walk**
Herb Orange, Ph.D.
Horticulture Department Chair
Clark Community College
Vancouver, Washington

    2.   **Adaptations in the Community Garden**
Leslie Phohl-Kosbau
Director, Community Gardens
Portland Parks and Recreation

    3.   **Nature Crafts: Simple Projects Especially Designed for the Long-term Care and Rehab Client**
Dana Ritsema, AC
Eloise Wiebe, AC

    4.   **Organizing the Basics for an Indoor, Year-round Gardening Program**
Teresia Hazen, HTR

5:00   CONFERENCE CONCLUDES
CERTIFICATES ISSUED

Program Planning Committee

Tom DeJardin, MSW, MPA
Administrator
Bishop Morris Care Center

Teresia Hazen, MA, HTR, Committee Chair
Registered Horticultural Therapist
Legacy Portland Hospitals

Kathy Kromm, BA
OSU Master Gardener
Legacy Extended Care Horticultural Therapy Volunteer

Erin LaRose, COTA/L
Certified Occupational Therapy Assistant
Legacy Extended Care

Priscilla Lane, RN
Legacy VNA

Nita Oliver, MN
OSU Master Gardener
Portland Parks & Recreation,
Community Gardens Board of Directors

Dana Ritsema, AC
Conference Program Assistant
Bishop Morris Care Center

Susan Sherborne, MS, CTRS
Certified Therapeutic Recreation Specialist
Legacy Extended Care

Catherine Van Son, RN, MSN
Staff Development Specialist
Legacy Extended Care

Eloise Wiebe, AC
Conference Program Assistant
Bishop Morris Care Center

Kevin Winslow, RN
Director of Nursing/Administrator
Emanuel Hospital Skilled Nursing Facility

Legacy Health System
Bishop Morris Care Center
2430 N.W. Marshall
Portland, Oregon 97210

ADAPTATIONS FOR ACCESSIBILITY

REGISTRATION

Name _____ Title _____

Company _____

Address _____

City _____ State _____ Zip _____

Phone (___) _____

	Early Bloomers Postmark by June 15	After June 15 Postmark	Please list fees
Workshop Registration	$45.00	$55.00	
Lunch - Salad Bar	$ 5.00	$ 5.00	
Nature Crafts Session	$ 5.00	$ 5.00	
		TOTAL.	

Legacy Health System cost center. _____

NOTE: Meal and Craft registration closes July 15th.

Pre-register for concurrent sessions. List the number of your choice.

A |___| D |___|
B |___| E |___|
C |___|

TEAMWORK WORKS! With two paid registrations at your workplace you may register a third person **FREE.** Photocopy registration form for each registrant. Team registration must be mailed together.

Make checks and purchase orders payable to Bishop Morris Care Center, Legacy Extended Care, 2430 NW Marshall, Portland, OR 97210.

Cancellations subject to $10.00 processing fee.
No refunds after July 17th.

Free Parking is available.
For further information, call Dana Ritsema at (503) 227-3791.

Printed with permission from Legacy Health System.

Status upon discharge

Cognition/perception: Patient is alert and oriented. Follows two-step directions.

Physical: Slight flexor tone noted with right elbow, otherwise flaccid. She can ambulate up to 30 feet using a wheeled walker with minimum assist. She needs help to keep the right hand on the walker. She requires fairly constant cues to shift weight to the left in order to free up the right lower extremity for swing through and occasional assist to advance and place the right foot.

Activities of daily living: Independent with setup from wheelchair with upper and lower extremity dressing, however pain management requires minimum to moderate assist. Transfer to toilet with minimum assist.

ANNUAL OUTLINE OF SAMPLE TOPICS AND PROJECTS

The following is a sample schedule of horticultural therapy gardening and nature crafts activities curriculum designed around the months and seasons. Bibliographies have been compiled for the nature crafts and horticulture program components. Patient interest and ability will determine many additional topics.

Each month includes such regular topics as: What's in bloom?, flower of the month study; literature and art, seed packet activities, study groups; and plant sales. Monthly curriculum materials are organized in three-ring binders. One-page study guides highlight monthly horticultural aspects of cultural celebrations and history. Study guides also focus on functional reading and cognitive skills development.

January
  Grow avocado pits
  Midwinter food tree for the birds

February
  Cut and force flowing branches
  Orange pomanders

March
  Start coleus and tomato seeds
  Dried flower table arrangements

April
Start cuttings for ivy topiaries
Make tussie mussie nosegays

May
Plant bean teepee
Pressing foliage and flowers

June
Floral arranging
Make a scarecrow for the garden

July
Propagate houseplant cuttings
Miniature floral arrangements

August
Transplant cool season crops
Make potpourri and sachets

September
Plant pansy seed
Chocolate leaf imprints for an ice cream party

October
Pot tulip bulbs for forcing
Stenciling with leaves for notebook/journal covers

November
Plant amaryllis
Vegetable stamps

December
Forcing narcissus
Pressed material tree/window ornaments

CONCLUSION

Horticultural therapy can be integrated into a skilled nursing facility, providing a wide scope and variety of program offerings to meet the needs, interests and abilities of seniors in physical rehabilitation. Therapy treatment teamwork enhances patient achievement of performance goals through highly meaningful and functional activities. The horticultural therapy program can create or enhance a positive facility culture and serve as a unique marketing tool in the health care system. Helping patients heal through contact with nature helps to provide balance in the high-tech, fast-paced hospital setting of this new managed care era.

REFERENCES

Morgan, B. (1989). *Growing together: Activities to use in your horticulture and horticultural therapy programs for children.* Pittsburgh: Pittsburgh Civic Garden Center.

Rothert, E.A., Daubert, J.R. (1981). *Horticultural therapy at a physical rehabilitation facility.* Glencoe, IL: Chicago Horticultural Society.

Implementing Horticultural Therapy into a Geriatric Long-Term Care Facility

Dee Liberatore McGuire

SUMMARY. This paper presents a personal account of how horticultural activities were implemented on a contractual basis in several nursing homes and later implemented through an activities therapy department. Individual examples are cited demonstrating the benefits of horticulture as a treatment modality offering an opportunity to assess functional levels and establish measurable goals and objectives. This paper shows how horticulture as an activity becomes respected as a therapy among disciplines of the care planning team at one long-term care facility. *[Article copies available for a fee from The Haworth Document Delivery Service: 1-800-342-9678. E-mail address: getinfo@haworth.com]*

I would like to share how I became involved with horticultural therapy for older adults. My degree is in fine arts and art education. I taught art to children, and was painting plants, seed pods and flowers when I developed a passion for growing plants and learning everything I could about them. Eventually, as a professional horticultural designer, I owned and operated an interior plant design and maintenance business and created indoor and outdoor topiary designs with my sculptor husband. After selling my interior plantscaping business, I wanted to do something more meaningful with my life. At that time my 71-year-old father became terminally ill. Since

Dee Liberatore McGuire, HTT, BFA, is Assistant Activities Director, Meridian Perring Parkway/Genesis Health Ventures.

Address correspondence to: 4021 Federal Hill Road, Jarrettsville, MD 21084.

[Haworth co-indexing entry note]: "Implementing Horticultural Therapy into a Geriatric Long-Term Care Facility." McGuire, Dee Liberatore. Co-published simultaneously in *Activities, Adaptation and Aging* (The Haworth Press, Inc.) Vol. 22, No. 1/2, 1997, pp. 61-80; and: *Horticultural Therapy and the Older Adult Population* (ed: Suzanne E. Wells) The Haworth Press, Inc., 1997, pp. 61-80. Single or multiple copies of this article are available for a fee from The Haworth Document Delivery Service [1-800-342-9678, 9:00 a.m. - 5:00 p.m. (EST). E-mail address: getinfo@haworth.com].

my mother was near 77, I assumed the role of primary care giver. Little did I realize the impact that experience would have in the years ahead.

While taking care of my father, it was obvious each day could be our last together. While we were all emotionally coming to terms with that reality, each day also provided the opportunity to share something which still involved life, enjoyment and hope. We enjoyed simple activities such as telling old stories, looking at photographs, reminiscing, welcoming family and friends, listening to music, sitting outside in the garden, and sharing with him my knowledge of the plants and flowers he received in many arrangements.

One of the floral arrangements he received while in the hospital contained three bare stems of corkscrew willow. We set up an experiment to see how long it would take them to root. The narrow vase was placed by the window near his bed. He and my mother checked on this periodically. When there were many roots, he said, "Plant this in your garden." Today, eight years later, it is a beautiful tree, well over 18 feet tall.

With hospice in place at my parents' home, the nurse, social worker and nursing assistants were surprised to see the attention my father gave to the pieces of nature I shared with him. For example, he was quite impressed with a miniature violet I gave him. He asked his visitors to count how many flowers were on the plant. He did this for a couple of weeks, and each time they came, they would check to see if another flower blossomed. Eventually, he gave the miniature violet to his special nurse. At first, she did not want to take it, but she realized it was important for her to accept this gift as his way of communicating his appreciation for her.

Eventually, my father did not want visitors or the television on, yet he still wanted to know when I was going to plant basil. It was May, so I set up the card table next to his bed, and he watched me separate the basil seeds from the dry flower spikes we had saved from the previous year's growth. He was too weak to sit up for long, but he managed to pick off some seeds and kept smelling them. He said, "I've never seen so many basil seeds in all my life. We should have a lot this year." The room was filled with the aroma of basil, and he requested spaghetti for dinner that night.

His sense of smell appeared to be heightened as his cancer spread and, at times, everything smelled bad to him. Before he was ill, he always enjoyed the smell of cloves. I put some clove oil on cotton balls and placed them around his room, he was able to tolerate this fragrance and it helped reduce the bad odor episodes.

My father and I shared many more interactions with nature's gifts while he was dying. The social worker from the hospice team asked if I had ever thought about working with the elderly. "Me? Not me! I'm taking care of my father; how would I do this for anyone else?" Sometimes we don't see the forest for the trees.

OFFERING HORTICULTURAL ACTIVITY SERVICES CONTRACTUALLY

Several months after my father's death, while teaching a course in the horticulture department at Dundalk Community College, in Baltimore, Maryland, I visited Keswick Adult Day Care Center. The college sponsored instructional programs for seniors there. The adult day care center was interested in a course combining art and nature crafts and the college offered to sponsor me as an instructor.

Shortly thereafter, I was asked to begin a program with the college's sponsorship at a local nursing home. However, I soon realized the college-sponsored curriculum was unrealistic because it required finished products and emphased craft techniques. Both the adult day care participants and the nursing home residents were far more responsive to working directly with the natural materials of plants, flowers, and herbs, etc. The dean overseeing those programs told me that the course would be dropped unless we did more arts and crafts and less horticulture. After completing the remaining instructional schedule of sessions for the college, I decided not to continue the next series.

Without the college sponsorship, I began contracting my horticultural activity services independently. At that time, staff from two more nursing homes in the area called me requesting horticultural programs for their residents.

In the spring of 1989, I attended a meeting/seminar of the American Horticultural Therapy Association at the Friends Psychiatric Hospital in Philadelphia. It was a very stimulating and affirming experience for me, and helped set the direction of my work in horticultural therapy.

Working now with the activities directors in three long-term nursing facilities, I adapted horticultural activities to fit the residents' needs and program budget. Sessions of one-and-one-half to two hours were scheduled weekly in each facility. Groups included a mixed functional level from low, moderate to more independent and were all called "Garden Club." Individual activities directors established the goals for each club. They were interested mainly in horticulture to provide benefits and opportunities to engage the residents cognitively, physically and psychosocially.

The horticultural activity included hands-on plant propagation, flower arranging, nature crafts, corsage making, smell and tell sessions, and some outdoor garden planting as well. Demonstrations of various planting techniques, observations of plant curiosities and seasonal natural materials provided opportunities for peer interaction and for relating to the wonders of nature within an otherwise boring environment. The activities staff, social worker and nursing staff often sat in during the session and took notes. Many were amazed at the responses from many of their more regressed residents.

One more nursing home was added to my schedule, and at each home the administrators were very supportive. I received a grant from Very Special Arts-Maryland and from the four Meridian nursing facilities–Hamilton, Cromwell, Homewood and Loch Raven. The grant supported a two-month special program with the residents called "Garden Club and Crafts." During the two-month period, I proposed to the activities department an outreach program that would include a one-to-one room visit using natural materials as sensory stimulation. Flowers, plants, herbs and other natural materials would be used to stimulate responses of the room-bound residents.

By 1991, my work as an independent horticultural activities specialist included ten individual nursing homes, one adult day care center, one congregate group home for older adults, and a plant appreciation course for seniors at Essex Community College in Baltimore, Maryland.

On a monthly basis, I conducted 32 sessions in the various nursing homes, documenting attendance and responses on a basic form that included the resident's name, verbal, physical, emotional responses and an area for comments. This information was used by the activities coordinators to meet treatment plans and goals for the residents. The program demonstrated this activity could be adapted to serve a variety of older adults and could easily be adapted for different levels of functioning as a therapeutic outreach modality in a long-term care facility.

I sensed it was time to focus on work in just one facility. I wanted to concentrate efforts, be part of an inter-disciplinary team, and take on the challenge of implementing an ongoing horticultural therapy program in one long-term care facility. I wanted to be trained to do all required paperwork, initial assessments, minimum data set and other care plan forms.

DEVELOPMENT OF A HORTICULTURAL THERAPY PROGRAM IN ONE GERIATRIC LONG-TERM CARE FACILITY

In August 1993, I was hired as Assistant Activities Director at Meridian Perring Parkway Nursing Facility (MPPNF) where I had been on contract for horticultural activities services three times per month for one year. The 130-bed, predominantly geriatric long-term care facility provides 24-hour nursing care, medical supervision, group and individual activities, and therapeutic diets. Social Services provide counseling, discharge, referral and placement. The facility offers rehabilitation through the physical therapy, occupational therapy, and speech therapy teams. Respite, short-stay care is also provided. Consultants are available, including a dentist, podiatrist, ophthalmologist, pharmacist and psychiatrist. The facility is Medicare-and Medicaid-certified. Community involvement is generated through the clergy, hospitals, schools, the business community and the Department of Aging. The philosophy of the institution is to provide quality care while creating a quality of life for every resident.

The administrator and activities director agreed a more consistent horticultural activities program would be an asset to the residents, staff and facility. They welcomed and supported the implementation of the program, already having seen the positive results of the monthly visits. The activities director wanted the residents to be motivated to come out of their rooms and out of the hallway to become passive or active participants in horticultural therapy activities. The activities director and I wanted to strengthen the existing activities calendar by offering a four-times-per-week horticultural therapy program. There would be two structured groups—flower arranging and garden club—and two room outreach programs. We agreed to try this for six months and then evaluate.

GENERAL PROGRAM GOALS

The general goals we wanted to achieve with the residents in the introduction of a four-times-per-week program were:

1. To increase and encourage socialization with peers, staff and volunteers;
2. To stimulate the senses through the use of natural materials;
3. To improve quality of life and self concept;
4. To maintain or increase present level of function;
5. To provide opportunities for reality orientation, validation and re-motivation;
6. To provide creative and first-time opportunities with plants and flowers;
7. To improve attention span and increase both mental and physical toleration during activity;
8. To observe nature and stimulate a sense of wonder and appreciation within the institutional environment;

9. To be involved with a meaningful failure-free activity;
10. To offer opportunity for communication and decision-making;
11. To stimulate response by eye movement, touch, smiles and gestures with the in-room horticulture therapy visits; and
12. To create an ongoing horticultural therapy outreach to our bedridden residents and hallway sitters.

As the sessions began, I was concerned about how residents would relate to seeing me daily, doing more than providing horticultural therapy. Would they continue to be motivated? Would my enthusiasm wane? Would I have the stamina to prepare the activities, escort residents, present the program, take notes and assist with returning residents and clean-up?–far more responsibility than my work as a contractor when residents were brought to activities with the tables already set up. Could I maintain quality sessions four times per week and still fulfill other job requirements as assistant activities director? Will I relate as a professional team player and a horticultural therapist? Will I earn the respect of the other disciplines? Would I learn to do all the required paperwork?

With these concerns in mind, I anticipated and looked forward to creating a quality program with the realistic limitations of space, budget and my other job requirements: Working with the social worker, rehabilitation team, the dietary and other staff; seeing results over the next few years; beautifying the courtyard and the grounds of the facility; educating the staff, families and volunteers about horticultural therapy benefits; learning how to assess and create individual treatment plans including horticultural therapy as a modality and; continued opportunities to improve the program and my own professional learning. A large job was ahead of me, but I looked forward to it. I often think about the quote by Theodore Roosevelt on my desk, "Do what you can with what you have where you are."

Within the first six months of the four-times-per-week schedule, the program was meeting activity therapy department goals. Because the supplies budget was only $40 per month, families and friends of the residents and other resources throughout the community were contacted for donations. They continue to contribute flowers, plants and supplies.

The activities director was supportive and flexible with scheduling, space utilization and training. Group attendance grew, and we could no longer meet in the activities room. Sessions were shifted to the dining room and living room. The administrator allocated monies for landscaping the grounds and improving the courtyard gardens. A volunteer garden club committee including residents, families, staff and volunteers was formed.

FEDERAL REGULATIONS AND REQUIRED PAPERWORK

At best, quality of life is an elusive concept subject to personal and individual definition, but a particular challenge arises when the phrase is attached to nursing homes. Basically, aged persons faced with the necessity for institutional care must cope with an enormous and painful range of losses. Dealt the multiple blows of debilitating infirmities, separation from family and friends, loss of home and personal possessions and, perhaps most importantly, loss of the ability to care for oneself, how is one to react? (Cohen, 1982, p. 4)

As part of my training during this time, I learned the Omnibus Budget Reconciliation Act (OBRA) was passed in 1987 and included language to improve and monitor the quality of lives of residents living in long-term care facilities in the US. OBRA guarantees residents in nursing facilities their rights under federal law. To the maximum extent possible, residents have authority to choose how to live their everyday lives and receive care subject to the facilities' rules affecting residents' conduct and regulations protecting residents' health and safety.

The Resident Assessment Instrument (RAI) is the federally mandated assessment tool developed by OBRA. RAI is an effective means of communication between disciplines—social work, nursing, activities therapy, physical, occupational, speech therapy, dietary—and is used for communication among nursing home shifts. The RAI includes Minimum Data Sets (MDS), Triggers, Resident Assessment Protocol (RAP) and Utilization Guideline. This information, and more, is found in residents' individual medical charts kept at the nursing station on each floor.

The activities therapy department is responsible for completing the Activity Pursuit and Patterns in the MDS and the Initial Activities History and Assessment for each resident. The assessment forms consistently reveal that residents enjoyed some involvement with plants, flowers or gardening in the past and might be receptive to the horticultural program. "The Winchester House Survey revealed that over 90 percent of residents had engaged in some form of gardening in the past" (Rothert & Daubert, 1981). This information has not been collected at MPPNF, but I estimate some 85 to 90% of residents had been gardeners.

Residents' strengths and weaknesses are better understood after the completion of the MDS. Then, as needed, care planning includes activity problems (if any), goals, approaches and an area for evaluation. During care planning sessions, we review with the other disciplines individual residents' activities, attendance records and participation levels including observations and notes on their specific involvement with horticulture.

Problems, goals, objectives and approaches involving horticultural activities as an intervention for many of our residents are documented.

DESCRIPTIONS OF HORTICULTURAL ACTIVITIES

Flower Arranging

Flower arranging meets on Monday afternoon; the average attendance is ten to fourteen residents. Some residents are escorted, some self-propel and others ambulate independently to the dining room. Low, moderate and independent levels of functioning are grouped together with two volunteers assisting. Sessions run about 60 to 90 minutes including cleanup. Residents arrange flowers in vases. Residents fill vases needing water. Flowers are placed in the middle of the table. Some flowers are pre-cut; others need cutting. Residents are offered therapeutic scissors (spring loaded or pressure release for those with limited hand function) or regular scissors.

The goal of this activity is to provide residents the opportunity to work with fresh flowers, adding beauty to the institutional environment while interacting psychosocially with peers and staff. Objectives for each resident at flower arranging sessions include:

- Touch and select flowers;
- Choose vase, scissors;
- Fill vase with water;
- Cut stems to fit vase;
- Complete one or more vases;
- Observe peers while tolerating being at activity for 20 minutes;
- Accept assistance from horticultural therapists, activities staff, or volunteers;
- Engage verbally with horticultural therapists and peers;
- Reminisce and share stories with group; and
- Decide what to do with flower arrangement.

Observations

Residents' skills using scissors have been observed over time. Some, who initially could not even hold scissors, are now cutting stems and flowers. This process is slow, but demonstrates of how horticulture as an activity becomes horticulture as a therapeutic tool. Flower arranging becomes a meaningful activity for the residents. They see an immediate positive result of their action, which reinforces their willingness to do it again. They are also stimulating interest among their peers who may be passively observing the flower arranging.

Flower arranging affords many opportunities for assessing problems and establishing goals for various functional levels. With more cognitively impaired residents, simple tasks can be established, observed and measured leading to long-range goals and solving problems and needs.

Over the past two years, seven to eight of the original group continue to do flower arranging. The more independent and higher functioning residents create three or four vases in one session. All who participate have a choice about what they will do with their arrangements. They may keep one for themselves, donate some for room-to-room visits conducted the next day or give one to their roommate.

The activities therapy department has received positive feedback about the flower arranging from other disciplines. MPPNF's director of nursing comments, "Horticultural therapy implementation in this facility has caused the need to re-evaluate cognitively impaired residents. Residents who were viewed as having great difficulty attempting to communicate or perform daily tasks have responded well in the flower arranging group." From the social worker at MPPNF, "All residents are enthusiastic about the horticulture program. It is interesting to me to see so many faces alert, smiling and bright when arranging flowers. It appears that their self-esteem grows and physical disabilities are diminished while they are participating in flower arranging. One of my most memorable moments was with a tall, lanky female resident of 84 years old with mental illness. She was so overcome with her ability to achieve such wondrous results in arranging various flowers that she would bring me in a vase of flowers each week for my desk. Her pride was so genuine that verbal communication was not necessary for her to express herself because her smiles and actions said it all."

Garden Club

Garden club meets once a week on Tuesday morning for about one hour. Additional time is given during fair weather months, late spring through early fall, when the group sometimes meets on Wednesday or Friday afternoons. The average attendance is ten to 12 residents. We meet in the dining room, activities room and courtyard garden. From the initial assessments of our residents, we find many have an interest in gardening or house plants, lived on a farm or have some past experience with plants. The residents wish to continue their contact with plants while they are in the nursing home. Garden club gives them the opportunity to have their hands in the soil, work with plants, plant seeds and watch things germinate and grow.

The goal of Garden Club is to provide residents the opportunity to work with plants and other natural materials in a relaxed setting while benefitting psychosocially, physically, emotionally and cognitively in an institutional setting. Objectives for each resident participating in garden club include:

- Focus attention on activity for 45 minutes to 60 minutes;
- Willingly try "new experience" with plants;
- Re-learn by repetition of tasks;
- Make choices and decisions about materials and methods of planting;
- Complete tasks sequentially by potting, plants, seeds, etc.;
- Select plants to be cared for as an independent project;
- Become aware of season and current weather;
- Cooperate with peers, volunteers and horticultural therapist;
- Recall past gardening experiences and share with group;
- Be stimulated by plant curiosities and nature's gifts;
- Work on plants indoors or outdoors as desired;
- Learn names of plants and methods of care and recall them between sessions;
- Share a leisure activity with friends and family; and
- Enhance self esteem by helping to beautify courtyard garden with planting planters.

Observations

The purchase of two mobile fluorescent light garden units, one in the dining room and one in the activities room, allows us to house many plants. The Tuesday morning garden club group has been very successful propagating a variety of plants rooted either in soil and/or water. When it comes to tending the light garden unit, the residents need assistance from me or a volunteer or staff member. They enjoy watering the plants and pruning them. Several residents have their own plants growing on their window sills in their rooms. We also use the window sills in the activity room.

In 1995, the garden club planted 14 hanging baskets and 10 large planters which were placed in the outdoor courtyard garden. In the beginning of spring, when it was too chilly to be outside, six large planters were brought inside in the dining room, tables were moved aside, drop cloths were placed on the floor, and four residents were positioned around each planter. The housekeeping, maintenance, dietary activities and nursing staff assisted in organizing this activity. Many residents who could not go outside because of the wind or breeze or chill were eager to plant indoors in the large planters.

Garden Club occasionally offers a good opportunity for the other disciplines to observe the residents in settings in which they can show some of their strengths by performing tasks. One of our care planning nurses states, "I have observed some very positive behaviors brought about by the introduction of horticultural therapy in the nursing home. So many of our residents had very active and fulfilling lives. I have often heard some say how they wished they had a job or some work to do. The activities done in the garden club give them an opportunity to feel they are working or making a positive contribution to the nursing home. In the spring and summer our 'work crew' loved getting their hands dirty planting flowers around the nursing home and in our courtyard. I heard residents debating with each other about the 'best' way to arrange flowers in the planters. One resident who is cognitively impaired and seldom spoke or showed interest in her environment took on the responsibility of planting various colors and types of flowers in a large planter. This chore took her well over an hour. When she was finished, she wiped the soil off her hands. Her eyes were bright and happy but not as bright as her sunny smile when everyone complimented her good job. This chore gave her such satisfaction and purpose. These results gave the staff much gratification."

Flower Visits—One to One

On Tuesday afternoon, horticultural therapy consists of taking flower arrangements to individuals in their rooms. This outreach is conducted bi-weekly between two floors. Twenty-five to thirty residents are visited during a one-and-a-half to two hour period. Many residents are bedridden. The time spent with each resident can vary from three to five minutes or longer. It is important to enter the room in a non-hurried manner and to give direct, full attention to the resident.

The flower arrangements created by the residents who participated in the Monday flower arranging session are used. Depending on the amount of flowers donated, between 30 to 35 vases are made. In addition, some flowers and vases are reserved on the cart for those residents who want to create their own. Those who do create their own often remark positively about their accomplishments.

The goal of the one-on-one flower visits is that residents will be stimulated cognitively, physically, emotionally and socially and respond to the horticultural therapist. The objectives of the flower visits are that residents will respond by:

- Admiring and observing the color, size and smell of the flowers;
- Recalling flowers or gardens in their past;
- Identifying names of flowers;
- Reaching for flowers and holding vase;
- Selecting flowers for vase;
- Placing flowers in vase appropriately;
- Being less lethargic, less restless, less distracted for two to three minutes;
- Turning body to see flowers;
- Altering anxious, sad or depressed mood;
- Being at ease with visit;
- Expressing feeling about relationships or past roles;
- Forming relationship of trust with horticultural therapist; and
- Accepting invitation to attend flower arranging group.

Observations

Room-to-room flower visits are a very important part of our horticultural therapy program. They offer the opportunity for the resident and horticultural therapist to form an ongoing relationship through the many stages of institutional living. The simple gift of a vase of flowers can be meaningful to the resident who is adjusting to placement. Flower visits are often responsible for involving residents in further participation in other horticultural activities. It is an appropriate activity to offer when residents decline in physical and mental health status. For the past three years, flower visits have also become a means to reach out to the dying resident. It is a rewarding area for those horticultural therapists interested in working with hospice, death and dying residents.

Sensory Stimulation Outreach

Sensory stimulation outreach is conducted early Thursday afternoon on a bi-weekly basis between two floors for one hour. In-room outreach is offered for 10 to 15 minutes to two individual residents. A small group of two to four residents meets in the hallway or residents' lounge for 15 to 20 minutes per session. The horticultural therapist selects individuals and forms small groups of compatible residents while controlling the amount of sensory stimulation offered.

The goal of sensory stimulation outreach is to provide residents opportunities to increase the use of their senses–smell, taste, touch, sight, sound and movement–by providing natural materials such as flowers, fruits and vegetables. The resident interacts with the horticultural therapist while enhancing time spent during waking hours. The sensory stimulation outreach program has the following objectives for residents:

- Increase physical response;
- Increase awareness of environment through reality orientation;
- Decrease loneliness by increased sharing with others;
- Respond by tasting;
- Touch and identify familiar objects, i.e., apple, orange, etc.;
- Respond to stimuli through eye movement, focus;
- Increase verbal response;
- Recall past events and feelings; and
- Increase interaction with horticultural therapist and activity staff.

Observations

Many of the residents with cognitive impairments respond to this form of horticultural therapy. Often, family visiting in rooms will need time to share their concerns with staff. They need to be informed about the behavioral expectations appropriate with sensory visits and that it may "be impossible for the patient to learn new material" or to recognize familiar objects or faces (Dale, McCloskey and Bulechek, 1994, p. 44).

People with dementia often have trouble screening out such distractions as television noise or other conversations. By regular, slow-paced visits, sensory stimulation can be geared to residents' cognitive abilities and interests. The horticultural therapist must have the amount of time necessary to establish a routine and trust. This area needs further development in our facility. The needs are becoming greater as the number of bedridden, acute care residents and residents with various forms of dementia grows.

Summary

The activities staff has a variety of job requirements that restrict the time available to spend with room and hallway visits. Due to budgetary restrictions, another staff person cannot be hired now. However, because horticultural therapy as an intervention for our residents' needs has made a positive impact in this facility, the administrator, activities director, and other disciplines all agree our future plans must include strengthening the horticultural therapy activities.

HORTICULTURAL THERAPY CARE PLAN–
THREE TYPICAL PROBLEMS FOUND IN MANY LONG-TERM
CARE FACILITIES

Problem Example #1

Problem: Diversional activity deficit related to depression as exhibited by apathy, withdrawal and refusal to leave room.

Long Term Goal: Resident will attend and regularly participate in Garden Club within 90 days.

Objectives: The resident will:

- Accept invitation to attend Garden Club once a week over the next 30 days;
- Help pass out supplies once per week over the next 30 days while attending Garden Club; and
- Respond to questions by the horticultural therapist during Garden Club once per session while also conversing with peers twice per session, once a week over the next 30 days.

Approaches:

- Horticultural therapist or activity staff will show the activity schedule of events each day to the resident and inform him/her about Garden Club sessions.
- Volunteer or activity staff will invite resident to see plants growing on light garden unit in dining room twice each week.
- Resident will be transported to Garden Club by horticultural therapist or volunteer to observe Garden Club.
- Resident will be reminded by volunteer or staff 30 minutes before Garden Club that session will be held and will offer transport assistance.

Evaluation: 30-60-90 days as needed.

Problem Example #2

Problem: Impaired mobility related to cerebral vascular accident as exhibited by limited endurance while ambulating and limited fine motor dexterity in hands.

Long Term Goal: Resident will ambulate to Garden Club and use scissors over the next 90 days.

Objectives: Resident will:

- Check on plants twice per week in dining room with assistance over the next 30 days;
- Ambulate to flower arranging once per week over the next 30 days;
- Demonstrate willingness to practice with therapeutic scissors of choice; and
- Plant one jade plant in clay pot, appropriately sequencing steps of task once over the next 30 days as an independent project in the activity room.

Approaches:

- Resident will be shown light unit in dining room by horticultural therapist twice weekly.
- Resident will be asked to check on plants by activities staff once or twice weekly.
- Activities staff or volunteer will inform resident of time and place for Garden Club and flower arranging.
- Activities staff or volunteer will offer assistance to resident while ambulating to garden club or flower arranging for first few visits.
- Activities staff will provide variety of therapeutic scissors and opportunity for experimentation.
- Horticultural therapist will escort resident to activities room for independent project and provide materials for planting.

Evaluations: 30, 60 or 90 days as needed.

Problem Example #3

Problem: Activity intolerance related to cognitive impairment as evidenced by difficulty in performing simple tasks, restlessness and refusal to leave room/hallway.
Long Term Goal: Resident will respond appropriately to one-to-one flower visits twice per week over the next 90 days.
Objectives: Resident will:

- Converse with horticultural therapist or volunteer for two minutes while receiving flowers once weekly over the next 90 days;
- Reach and choose from flowers offered once weekly over the next 90 days;
- Change facial expression while smelling flowers once or twice weekly over the next 90 days; and

- Express appreciation to horticultural therapist or volunteer when receiving flowers.

Approach:

- Horticultural therapist or volunteer will visit residents in room or hallways while presenting flowers.
- Horticultural therapist or volunteer will ask resident to select one vase of flowers.
- Horticultural therapist will ask questions about flowers, gardens, etc., to encourage verbal response.

Evaluation: 30, 60 or 90 days

Horticultural Therapy Meeting Individual Treatment Goals: A Case Study

Mrs. A. is a 61-year-old female who sustained a cerebral aneurysm. She was alert; could not ambulate alone; had no sense of balance; had some expressive aphasia; and had a flat affect (i.e., lacked facial expression). Based on her diagnosis, it appeared there was brain damage. She was not expected to regain normal function with walking, talking or completing simple tasks. She would often answer "yes" to no questions and turn her head away when spoken to. She did not want to leave her room except to sit in the hallway. During one-to-one flower visits, in her first week of admittance, Mrs. A. did respond to me as I pushed the flower cart near her room. She smiled slightly while staring at a vase of carnations. As I reached to show her the flowers, I asked if she would like them for her night stand. She said, "Nice."

Her initial activity assessment, completed with her brother's assistance, indicated she had always had a garden and house plants. The MDS triggered activity problems. That information, plus her receptiveness to the first one-to-one flower visits, helped me to create a care plan for Mrs. A.

Problem: Activities intolerance related to cognitive impairment due to cerebral aneurysm as evidenced by impaired ability to ambulate, maintain a standing position, difficulty in performing simple tasks and refusal to leave room.

Goals for Mrs. A. Resident will:

- Accept invitation to horticultural activity once a week over the next 90 days;

- Observe peers or participate while at flower arranging twice per month over the next 90 days; and
- Smile, nod and respond verbally while at Garden Club twice per month over the next 90 days.

Approaches:

- Activities staff will visit resident daily to gain support and show calendar of events.
- Horticultural therapist will invite and assist resident to flower arranging or Garden Club.
- Staff will provide praise and encouragement while at horticultural activities and when resident returns to her room.

Evaluation: During the first 30 days, the resident attended and passively observed flower arranging and garden club but stayed for the entire session with some verbal (few word) responses. During the next 60 days we observed Mrs. A. during flower arranging. She did not yet put flowers in the vase, but held a flower for the entire session. No one criticized her, and she would leave with the flower in her hand.

One day, while attending flower arranging, she picked up the vase and began to drink the water. She accepted my reach to retrieve the vase while a volunteer brought her a glass of water. After drinking from the glass, she set it down. She picked up some flowers and put them down and watched for a while. Next to her were some cut stems another resident had clipped. She picked them up one by one and placed them in the drinking cup. I observed her during this time as she very careful and methodically put six or seven stems in the drinking cup. Next, she reached for a flower and placed it in the vase. While we cleared the table and cleaned up, she handed me both the flower in the vase and the drinking cup of stems.

This occurred about 90 days after the first care planning session. The resident had met the goals. New goals and approaches were planned, and Mrs. A. attained these within three months. She now regularly attended garden club and flower arranging, as well as other activities such as bake class and current events. She used scissors, which she had not been able to hold initially, and arranged several flowers in a vase each session.

In garden club, she was able to pot a cutting sequentially, something she had not been able to do when first admitted to the nursing home. To our amazement, she continually improved many functional levels. Cognitively, she was reading and writing. Physically, she was standing and pushing her wheelchair throughout the facility. Socially, she was interacting and speaking in sentences. Emotionally, she was laughing, smiling and giving direct eye contact.

Mrs. A. told me she was very bored with her wheelchair. However, she was still tiring easily and could not stand for long. At care planning, I asked physical therapy to evaluate Mrs. A. for the use of a merriwalker. The other disciplines agreed, and physical therapy arranged for her to borrow a merriwalker from another facility. The merriwalker became a link through which Mrs. A. gained more independence, strength and self esteem. In three to four months, she was going around the facility, assisting other residents, using the elevator by herself and resting in the merriwalker as needed. She was strengthening her legs, and was able to pick up the cross bar on the merriwalker and walk away from it for short periods of time.

Mrs. A. had been in our facility for one year when we began planting the outdoor courtyard planters. While she was participating in this outdoor activity, she picked up the cross bar from the merriwalker and began to push it away. I kept my eye on her as she approached the planter she chose to work on. We watched her pick up geraniums from the table and place them in the planter. She completed this large planter standing alone without the merriwalker and was very proud. Several months later, Mrs. A. was discharged to an assisted living apartment.

Horticulture as an Activity Now Viewed as Therapy

Horticulture as an activity in our facility has come to be viewed as a therapy among disciplines of the care planning team. One of our care planning nurses reported, "One of my biggest concerns is our bedridden residents. In-room horticultural therapy has brightened their lives for a few moments several times a week. I have seen these residents smile at the beauty of the flower, speak about their own gardens, touch the different textures of flowers and share some quality one-to-one time with our therapist."

Our physical therapist commented that the horticultural program promotes neuromuscular functioning directly and indirectly. Directly, it promotes the use of limbs to propel chairs or to ambulate to the activity. To participate in the activity, residents use limbs to stand, reach, lean forward, pick up, cut, etc. It stimulates the use of the imagination to create a design or to recognize an odor, and it stimulates cognition via recall and socialization. Indirectly, horticultural therapy activity distracts patients' focus from self, facilitates balance and increases strength and endurance.

The occupational therapist and his/her assistant observes the sessions. Recently, an 89-year-old resident who had dislocated her left shoulder was being seen daily by the occupational therapist for the maximum amount of time allowed by insurance (six weeks for 30 minutes per session). Her goal was to exercise and use the left upper extremity area. The occupational therapist coordinated with me, and we came up with particular small tasks for the resident to do while achieving the therapeutic challenge of using her left upper extremity. We placed a flower pot on telephone books so she had to raise her arm higher to put soil in it or pot the plant. I suggested cleaning a tall plant while seated, requiring her to reach up. She was able to judge when she was fatigued and could not continue, but worked as much as safely possible in order to strengthen her shoulder. Occupational and activities therapy departments together continue to work with this resident to develop specific adaptations, and we look forward to cooperation with other rehabilitation teams as time and billing allows.

CONCLUSION

At a meeting in November 1995 sponsored by the Maryland Activity Coordinators' Society, Inc., I learned the Health Care Financing Administration (HCFA) of the Department of Health and Human Services recently created the new MDS 2.0 for long-term care facilities in the United States. All states are required to implement this new form by January 1, 1996. Horticultural therapists involved with horticulture as a modality of treatment in long-term care facilities will be interested to note that in Section N, Activity Pursuit Patterns, #4, General Activity Preferences adapted to residents current abilities, a Section "N" called "Gardening or Plants" can be checked off as preferences whether or not the activity is currently available to the resident.

Future research could compile data on how many residents in geriatric long-term care facilities prefer gardening or plants as a general activity preference as found in Section N, Activity Pursuit Patterns of the 1996 MDS 2.0.

We are reaching the goal-setting process in long-term care. Now more than ever, the time has arrived for us, as horticultural therapists, to educate and continue to impact this therapeutic milieu in geriatric long-term care.

REFERENCES

Cohen, Sylvia R. (1982). Quality of life as a way of life. *American Health Care Association Journal, 8.*

Dale, McCloskey & Bulechek. (1994, Jan./Feb.) Nursing Interventions Classification Use in Long-Term Care. *Geriatric Nursing, Volume 15, Number 1.*

Robert, E.A. and Daubert, J.R. (1981). *Horticultural Therapy for Nursing Homes, Senior Centers and Retirement Living.* Glencoe, IL: Chicago Horticultural Society.

Special skills needed when communicating with the Alzheimer's patient. (1995, November/December). *Newsletter of the Alzheimer's Association, Baltimore/ Central Maryland Chapter.*

A Horticultural Therapy Program for Individuals with Acquired Aphasia

Martha Taylor Sarno
Nancy Chambers

SUMMARY. A horticultural therapy program designed for individuals with acquired aphasia, a communication impairment characterized by difficulty in speaking and understanding speech, is described. Nineteen patients ranging in age from 49 to 90 years of age (mean 73.9) participated in the project. The program consisted of structured activities designed to provide a well-rounded introduction to plant care as a leisure time or avocational activity. More than half of the patients reported that they began to care for plants which were acquired in the project at home. Some participants became volunteers in the greenhouse. Those who participated were observed to increase their verbal behavior and social interaction, and their family members reported a noticeable increase in patient gratification. *[Article copies available for a fee from The Haworth Document Delivery Service: 1-800-342-9678. E-mail address: getinfo@haworth.com]*

INTRODUCTION

A fundamental philosophical basis for horticultural therapy is the belief that contact with plants meets a basic human psychological need. It recog-

---

Martha Taylor Sarno, MA, MD (hon), is Professor, Clinical Rehabilitation Medicine, New York University School of Medicine and Director, Speech-Language Pathology Department, Rusk Institute of Rehabilitation Medicine, New York University Medical Center.

Nancy Chambers, HTR, is Supervisor, Enid A. Haupt Garden, Rusk Institute of Rehabilitation Medicine, New York University Medical Center.

[Haworth co-indexing entry note]: "A Horticultural Therapy Program for Individuals with Acquired Aphasia." Sarno, Martha Taylor and Nancy Chambers. Co-published simultaneously in *Activities, Adaptation and Aging* (The Haworth Press, Inc.) Vol. 22, No. 1/2, 1997, pp. 81-91; and: *Horticultural Therapy and the Older Adult Population* (ed: Suzanne E. Wells) The Haworth Press, Inc., 1997, pp. 81-91. Single or multiple copies of this article are available for a fee from The Haworth Document Delivery Service [1-800-342-9678, 9:00 a.m. - 5:00 p.m. (EST). E-mail address: getinfo@haworth.com].

nizes that people created and used gardens, since early times, for both restorative and educational purposes. Horticultural therapy based on the "sharing of the experience of plants between the therapist and patient/client" (Relf, 1992) offers discrete benefits to individuals which can enhance and augment their rehabilitation. This paper details the objectives, implementation and results of a pilot horticultural therapy program organized for patients with aphasia at the Howard A. Rusk Institute of Rehabilitation Medicine.

THE NATURE OF APHASIA

Over one million individuals in the United States have acquired aphasia, a communication disorder which is characterized by difficulty in speaking and understanding speech (NIH, 1979). Aphasia is usually the result of a stroke, but head injuries and brain tumors are also causative. The majority of strokes occur in middle-aged and elderly individuals. In the United States, this population is predicted to reach 31 million people by the year 2000 and may reach 22 percent of the total population by the year 2030. The number of individuals with aphasia can thus be expected to increase significantly (Spencer, 1984).

Aphasia is the result of damage to speech and language centers in the dominant, usually the left, hemisphere of the brain. The brain injury is most commonly the result of a disturbance in the circulation of blood to the involved area due to a clot in or rupture of a key blood vessel.

In general, different types of aphasia correlate with different locations of cerebral lesions and may be classified according to their primary characteristics, especially those involving speech production. Aphasia can be so mild that the symptoms are barely perceptible or so severe that the person is unable to speak, write or read effectively. The two most common categories of aphasia are fluent aphasia and nonfluent aphasia.

Patients with nonfluent aphasia may have limited vocabulary; slow, hesitant and effortful speech; awkward articulation; and a restricted use of grammar. Speech comprehension is generally normal or near normal. Patients with nonfluent aphasia tend to express themselves in vocabulary that is restricted to nouns, verbs, adjectives and adverbs. Prepositions, articles, and conjunctions (the little words which provide the grammar of the language) are generally lacking. Individuals with nonfluent aphasia tend to be aware of their communication deficiencies and usually have impaired motor function of the right arm and leg (i.e., right hemiplegia or paresis).

Patients with fluent aphasia generally have easily articulated speech produced at a normal rate, with preserved melody. They tend to have the greatest difficulty in retrieving nouns and verbs. They may also have a limited awareness of their difficulty in communication. They generally do not have physically disabilities, since their lesions are usually located in the posterior portion of the brain distant from motor areas. *Fluent aphasia* is also characterized by impaired auditory comprehension. When fluent aphasia is severe, word and sound substitutions may be of such magnitude and frequency that speech may be rendered meaningless.

When aphasia is severe and there is marked dysfunction in all language modalities (speaking, understanding speech, reading, and writing), it is referred to as global aphasia. Global aphasia is not a type of aphasia but a designation of severity.

If a patient is fortunate enough to fully recover from aphasia, it generally occurs within hours or days following onset. When aphasia persists for several weeks or months, individuals rarely return to their previous level of communication effectiveness. The abrupt onset of aphasia initiates a series of reactions that may have an impact on every aspect of daily life. The ability to cope with being socially different, feelings of loss, lowered self esteem and possible changes in vocational status may pose serious, seemingly insurmountable, problems to the individual with aphasia. Personal accounts of aphasia make it clear that an individual's identity may change after the onset of aphasia. Roles and responsibilities in the family may no longer apply. Not only may role changes bring about a "loss of self," but the family is also strained as the aphasic person, who may once have controlled the family's social and financial life, must give up these roles (Sarno, 1993).

SPEECH/LANGUAGE REHABILITATION

Speech therapy provided by speech-language pathologists is the basis for most of the language rehabilitation offered to individuals with aphasia. These services are usually rendered in rehabilitation centers, and in hospitals by speech-language pathologists in private practice. In large, comprehensive treatment centers, aphasia rehabilitation is offered through both individual and group therapy.

Two of the most difficult aspects of managing patients with aphasia are its chronic nature and long, arduous recovery process. The recovery timetable is variable, but a gradual improvement usually takes place over many months. For a substantial number of patients, the process takes several years.

Speech therapy addresses the communication problems caused by aphasia and includes educating the patient and family about the nature of the condition. Therapy also focuses on Aphasia's significant psychosocial impact on the individual and family. Social isolation is one of the most common consequences of aphasia, and a substantial depression may be the most important reaction for many. Communication is an essential human behavior that, if impaired, may result in frustration, decreased self-esteem, and a decreased sense of personhood (Sarno, 1986, 1993).

THE HOWARD A. RUSK INSTITUTE OF REHABILITATION MEDICINE

The Howard A. Rusk Institute of Rehabilitation Medicine is the clinical facility of the Department of Rehabilitation Medicine of the New York University School of Medicine. It was the first university-related rehabilitation hospital in the country and is the world's largest university affiliated center for the treatment of disabled adults and children. Founded by Dr. Rusk in 1947, the Institute has a long history of providing comprehensive and innovative rehabilitation to individuals with a wide range of physical disabilities. On average, 1000 inpatients and 8500 outpatients, both children and adults, are treated annually.

THE RUSK INSTITUTE GLASS GARDEN

Among the unique features of the Rusk Institute is the Glass Garden built in 1958 with a generous gift from Mrs. Enid A. Haupt. It is a 1700-square foot conservatory and the centerpiece of a 12,000-square foot greenspace consisting of an outdoor perennial garden, a children's "playgarden," and indoor displays which include orchids, palms, bromeliads and other tropical plants adaptable to New York offices and apartments. It also includes an aquatic garden with fish, turtles and a medley of tropical birds. The Glass Garden was the first facility of its kind designed to be totally accessible to people in wheelchairs. It serves as a model for organizations designing similar facilities across the country and hosts more than 100,000 visitors annually.

The Glass Garden serves the important restorative function of providing patients, their visitors, and hospital staff a place to escape the rigors of clinical life. The garden is also a setting in which patients, both old and young, work with trained horticultural therapists on activities designed to improve physical and cognitive functioning and achieve a sense of personal accomplishment, productivity and independence. Over 3000 horticultural therapy sessions are rendered annually.

Patients, referred by their occupational therapists, attend daily, hour-long sessions in the garden in intergenerational groups. They propagate seeds and cuttings, arrange flowers, make cactus gardens and terrariums, and also work on various horticultural craft projects. All patients have their own bench space in the greenhouse, and they take their plants home upon discharge. The horticultural activities are designed to meet the patients' treatment goals in both functional and cognitive areas.

In addition, the horticultural therapy program offers other discrete benefits to individuals participating in the garden program. Recent studies show gardens, by their very nature, have remarkable restorative effects by causing feelings to shift to a more positive state. The color green, for example, is associated with equilibrium, peace and comfort, and passive involvement with gardens has been shown to reduce stress and depression, increase concentration, and increase the ability to focus attention (Kaplan, 1989; Relf, 1992).

Along with the nostalgic and reminiscent benefits inherent in gardens, plants and flowers engage all of the senses—sight, sound, touch, smell and taste—at once. Indeed, "a rose is a rose is a rose" even without the ability to communicate. The colors, textures, and scents are a universal language; contrast the lemon verbena with the tomato scent, the texture of lambs' ears to geraniums. One feels the sun's heat and warmth on one's arms and hears the babbling water and the birds. These sensory elements can be readily perceived and appreciated.

Gardening is one of the most popular avocational activities in the United States for older adults (Gardens for All, 1979). Books, television programs, botanic gardens, classes, and clubs are devoted to promoting and teaching about gardens and related activities. Participation in horticultural activities can increase an individual's opportunity to meet and socialize with others in an area of shared and common interest.

A major portion of self-esteem derives from what a person can actually do and the degree of control they have in the decision-making process. Horticultural activities are very diverse and offer the individual tangible results and end-products which have value to others. Gardening and house plant care activities can function as a work substitute and encourage decision-making: Do I grow flowers or vegetables? Do I want pink or yellow? Do I prune today or repot? Do I water today or tomorrow?

THE RUSK INSTITUTE APHASIA COMMUNITY
GROUP PROGRAM

The Aphasia Community Group (ACG) established at the Rusk Institute of Rehabilitation Medicine in 1987 was one of the first groups organized in response to the National Aphasia Association (NAA) mandate to develop a national support network. It is a socialization/recreation program designed to provide conversational and social opportunity for patients with aphasia who are no longer receiving speech-language pathology services. Volunteer leaders who are trained by the Rusk professional staff conduct the four different Aphasia Community Group weekly meetings. Meetings are structured around specific activities to foster conversational and social skills (e.g., discussion of current events).

The National Aphasia Association (NAA) was established in 1987 to act as an informational resource for individuals with aphasia, their families, and professionals. The NAA informs the public about the nature of aphasia and its impact to increase an awareness and understanding of the condition. Educational materials, a newsletter, and a national support network for the aphasia community are among its ongoing activities. An effort to focus public attention on aphasia is conducted annually in June.

There are currently over 150 individual aphasia support groups called Aphasia Community Groups (ACG) around the nation. Some are hospital based, but the majority are community based. The NAA has been the benefactor of a major federally-funded study of *Quality of Life after Stroke,* awarded to the Rehabilitation Institute of Chicago. This funding has made it possible to prepare and distribute a manual on creating new aphasia community groups and enrich existing groups, as well as to install an 800-line which responds to an average of 300 telephone calls each month.

A PILOT HORTICULTURAL THERAPY PROGRAM FOR PEOPLE WITH APHASIA

A pilot horticultural therapy program was organized for patients in the ACG Program in the spring and summer of 1994. Individuals with aphasia and their significant others were invited to participate. The Pilot Horticulture Program for patients in the ACG Program was designed to:

1. Provide a well-rounded introduction to horticulture as a leisure activity;
2. Engage in horticultural activities which have avocational values;
3. Decrease stress;
4. Increase self esteem; and
5. Provide conversational and social opportunity.

Nineteen patients (11 male/8 female) with aphasia participated in the study. They ranged from 49 to 90 years of age (mean 73.9) and had acquired aphasia between 1.5 to 13.5 years earlier (mean 4.3). Of those subjects with aphasia resulting from a stroke, three had fluent aphasia and 13 had nonfluent aphasia. The aphasia severity ranged from individuals who were initially unable to communicate using speech to those who manifest mild communication deficits to those who had global aphasia. Thirteen of the patients were unemployed at the time of the stroke. The patients had been employed in a wide variety of occupations (e.g., attorney, physician, financial advisor, secretary, homemaker, wholesaler) (Table 1).

Four groups of patients and spouses participated in the program and met three different times over an eight-week period (Table 2). The focus of the program centered on the patients' abilities and on social activities utilizing horticulture that were productive, educational, engaging and rewarding.

The Pilot Horticultural Program for Aphasia consisted of structured activities aimed at providing a well-rounded introduction to plant care as a leisure time or avocational activity. Opportunities for the pursuit of shared activities with family members and friends were highlighted. The activities were selected for their potential for reducing stress and/or increasing self-esteem and were structured to encourage decision-making and autonomy. Care was taken to provide both visual and verbal demonstration of each activity.

Each hour-long session, conducted by a horticultural therapist, included approximately six participants. The classes were dedicated to a variety of horticultural activities that were complex, yet easily broken down into single-step increments:

1. Plant propagation included activities involving various methods for growing new plants from stem cuttings, single node cuttings, division and simple repotting. The participants, patients and spouses, had a selection of plants from which to choose. The finished products were brought home.
2. Small (five-inch) container cactus gardens were made by mixing the proper soil components, choosing the individual plants for the garden, transplanting the small cactus and succulents, and finishing the project with sand and rocks. Each garden was brought home.
3. Fresh flower arrangements were created and brought home.
4. A kitchen gardening session included looking at many diverse plants grown from seeds and pits (date palm, grapefruit, coffee, macadamia plant, coconut palm) and selecting one to propagate. The fruits were all cut, shared, and eaten before propagation. The projects were all brought home to grow.

TABLE 1. Aphasia Community Group Horticultural Program
MAY/JUNE 1994

MEMBER	SIGNIFICANT OTHER IN ATTENDANCE	AGE	YRS SINCE ONSET OF APHASIA	OCCUPATION
M.A.	attendant	72	3	secretary
J.A.	–	49	3	financial advisor
B.B.	–	67	1.5	haircutter
E.C.	attendant	90	2	receptionist/secretary
B.F.	attendant	80	4	antique dealer/retailer
I.F.	attendant	84	3	attorney
R.G.	spouse	79	7	physician (ob–gyn)
H.G.	spouse	68	3	watchmaker
Z.G.	attendant	68	4	housewife
H.I.	spouse	80	5	wholesale sportswear market
R.J.	–	81	2.5	secretary
K.K.	spouse	75	3	housewife
B.M.	–	82	5	accountant
K.M.	–	66	5	wholesale fabric market
M.M.	–	80	3.5	corporate executive
L.S.	spouse	65	5	editorial assistant
H.S.	attendant	90	2	wholesale trimming market
D.S.	–	80	6	wholesale button market
F.T.	–	49	13.5	teacher (1st grade)

RESULTS AND DISCUSSION

The Horticultural Program for Aphasia proved to be popular with both patients and family members. All who attended expressed enthusiasm for the program and pleasure in participation. No one dropped out of the program and attendance was high. Patients without aphasia who learned of the program inquired about possible participation.

Many patients and spouses asked that the program be repeated annually

TABLE 2. Participation–Aphasia Community Group Horticultural Program.

MAY/JUNE 1994

TUESDAY		
	M.A.	attendant
	B.B.	
Group I and II	R.G.	spouse
May 10 (tour)	H.G.	spouse
	K.K.	spouse
	L.S.	spouse
	D.S.	
	F.T.	
Group I	B.B.	
May 17-June 21	H.G.	spouse
	L.S.	spouse
	F.T.	
Group II	M.A.	attendant
May 24-June 28	R.G.	spouse
	K.K.	spouse
	D.S.	

THURSDAY		
	J.A.	
Group III	E.C.	attendant
May 19(tour)	B.F.	attendant
May 26-June 30	Z.G.	attendant
	K.M.	
	H.S.	attendant

FRIDAY		
Group IV	I.F.	attendant
May 13 (tour)	H.I.	spouse
May 20-June 24	R.J.	
	B.M.	
	M.M.	

Group I	4 patients	2 spouses	–	
Group II	4 patients	2 spouses	1 attendant	
Group III	6 patients	–	4 attendants	
Group IV	5 patients	1 spouse	1 spouse	

as a regular part of the Aphasia Community Program. More than half of those who attended reported they began to care for plants which were acquired in the pilot project at home. Some of the spouses and the volunteer leaders observed that many of the individuals with aphasia appeared to do more talking while engaged in horticultural activities. One spouse indicated that houseplants became a newly shared hobby with her partner. Two of the participants with aphasia are now volunteers in the Glass Garden as a result of their experience in the pilot program.

Most endeavors require some degree of verbal skill, and it is always a challenge to find recreational and avocational activities which are suitable for individuals with aphasia. Clearly, the nature of horticultural activities lend themselves easily to communicative disabled individuals. In the horticultural context, the lack of demand for verbal interaction reduces the burden on the disabled communicator, thereby relieving stress and facilitating relaxation and pleasure. This is believed to foster the increased talking observed by spouses and volunteers. Contact with living plants and natural materials provides soothing and comforting sensory involvement. The enjoyment and satisfaction expressed by the patients reflect this. The possibility of creating environments in which houseplants can thrive under the patient's nurturing care can bring gratification and reward to the individual. This is revealed by the continued horticultural therapy participation of patients who became volunteers, and by the increased socialization and verbalizations of patients we observed. Family members also reported patient gratification.

The Rusk Institute pilot horticultural project has opened up new and exciting possibilities for further application in providing support and socialization to individuals with aphasia. The horticultural activity seemed to also stimulate the use of related vocabulary, e.g., enthusiasm for horticulture therapy may facilitate the use of associated words such as flower, leaf, etc. We hope to gain new experience with this tool and develop other models of horticultural activity for individuals with communication disorders. The Pilot Horticultural Program was not designed as a research project, therefore, outcome data are not available. A method for collecting such outcome information is included in the planned replication of this project.

REFERENCES

Gardens for All, Inc. (1978). *Gardening in America.* Burlington, Vermont.

Kaplan, R. and Kaplan, S. (1989). *The Experience of Nature.* New York: Cambridge University Press.

National Institute of Health. (1979). *Aphasia: Hope Through Research.* National Institutes of Health Publication No. 80-391, Bethesda, MD: NIH.

Relf, D. (ed.). (1992). *The role of horticulture in human well-being and social development.* Portland: Timber Press.

Sarno, M.T. (1993). Aphasia rehabilitation: Psychosocial and ethical considerations. *Aphasiology, 7(4)*, 321-334.

Sarno, M.T. (1986). *The silent minority: The patient with aphasia.* Hemphill Lecture. Chicago: Rehabilitation Institute of Chicago.

Spencer, G. (1984). *Projections of the population of the United States by age, sex, and race: 1983 to 2030.* Current Population Reports, Series P-25, No. 952. Washington, DC: US Bureau of the Census.

Alleviating Stress
for Family Caregivers of Frail Elders
Using Horticultural Therapy

Deborah J. Smith
Philip McCallion

ABSTRACT. For elders living in the community who need assistance, most care is provided by family and friends. For many family caregivers this is a rewarding experience. For others, caregiving can be stressful. Few therapeutic services to help caregivers are available in the home, are flexible to caregiving time demands, support the time caregivers need for themselves or provide opportunities for joint activities for caregivers and care recipients. A Caregiver Horticulture Program is presented which addresses all of these needs. The components of the program are described, along with strategies for successful intervention. Finally, two case studies demonstrate implementation of the program. *[Article copies available for a fee from The Haworth Document Delivery Service: 1-800-342-9678. E-mail address: getinfo@haworth.com]*

INTRODUCTION

Horticultural therapists are most often associated with hospital and vocationally-based programs. However, a review of the affiliations of

Deborah J. Smith, RNCS, MEd, HTT, is Faculty Member, Ellis Hospital School of Nursing, Schenectady, NY.

Philip McCallion, PhD, is Research Associate, Ringel Institute of Gerontology, School of Social Welfare, University at Albany, Albany, NY.

[Haworth co-indexing entry note]: "Alleviating Stress for Family Caregivers of Frail Elders Using Horticultural Therapy." Smith, Deborah J., and Philip McCallion. Co-published simultaneously in *Activities, Adaptation & Aging* (The Haworth Press, Inc.) Vol. 22, No. 1/2, 1997, pp. 93-105; and: *Horticultural Therapy and the Older Adult Population* (ed: Suzanne E. Wells) The Haworth Press, Inc., 1997, pp. 93-105. Single or multiple copies of this article are available for a fee from The Haworth Document Delivery Service [1-800-342-9678, 9:00 a.m. - 5:00 p.m. (EST). E-mail address: getinfo@haworth.com].

American Horticultural Therapy Association members indicates that horticultural therapists are a diverse group, frequently hold additional professional credentials, and practice in varied settings. As what they do is increasingly understood and valued, they are being called upon to adapt their programs to address unique needs in environments that do not always lend themselves to large scale horticulture activities. This article will highlight services to one such group, in-home family caregivers of frail and chronically ill elderly persons, and explain how services may be delivered in family homes. It will also illustrate how horticultural therapy skills are being increasingly included in the repertoires of varied professions.

BACKGROUND

Family members provide most long-term care for frail elderly persons living in the community. Estimates of the number of family members caring for aging spouses and parents range as high as 13.3 million (Stone & Kemper, 1989). The kinds of help they provide vary. For the purposes of this article, we are most interested in the 1.8 to 2.25 million persons estimated to provide help to aging family members in meeting basic activities of daily living (ADL) such as toileting and bathing, and the 2.4 million persons estimated to provide assistance with such instrumental activities of daily living (IADL) as transportation and shopping (Gevalnik & Simonsick, 1993; Stone, Cafferata, & Sangl, 1987). We chose this group because it is likely that the types of care provided place demands on the caregiver daily, and impact upon the caregiver's ability to do other things they value.

Providing care for an elderly family member can be very rewarding (Lawton, Kleban, Moss, Rovine, & Glicksman, 1989). For some caregivers, it is an opportunity to demonstrate their love for the aging care recipient, and to return the favor of caring and support provided by the care recipient in earlier times. Others draw strength from knowing that no one else can provide the same quality of care that they do. However, caregiving can also be a strain to many family members who provide assistance with ADL and IADL concerns. Some caregivers report an increase in back injuries and other physical problems, loss of energy and disrupted sleep patterns which decrease their effectiveness. This is particularly true for spouse caregivers who may already be in poor health themselves. Other caregivers become depressed and experience other psychosocial symptoms. Caregiving is also reported to affect job performance and career aspirations. Adult child caregivers, in particular, have indicated they are compelled to rearrange work schedules, change from full-time to part-time work, or terminate employment entirely. They also report conflict with caregiving responsibilities for their own dependent children (for a review of the positive and negative effects found for caregivers, see Toseland, Smith, & McCallion, 1995).

Many caregivers also acknowledge growing isolation as caregiving for a spouse or parent continues (Zarit, Orr, & Zarit, 1985). For some, the physical care and supervision needs of the person they care for means that they have had to give up work or personally satisfying recreation activities, because they cannot be fitted into the growing care regime. Others, often believing that no one else can match the care that they can provide, deny their own need for contacts with friends and family, and devote themselves to caregiving tasks. The end result is the same. Physical and psychological strains for the caregiver are compounded, as contacts with potential resources and support are lost. As one caregiving spouse stated: "We used to go out so much and did so many things together with our friends. I miss those days, it would be great to get out of the house, but I couldn't leave him with someone else, so we're both trapped here."

A growing range of services and supports are designed to bridge this growing chasm between family caregivers and their informal supports. The most popular option is the organization of groups, frequently consisting of other caregivers, to provide support. There are three major categories of supportive groups: mutual support groups, psychoeducational groups, and social, recreational and educational groups.

Mutual support groups help caregivers cope with the stresses of caregiving. The members share similar concerns. This shared experience helps the group to offer members understanding, information, and mutual aid; serve as a resource for social contacts; and help caregivers expand their range of friends and supporters. Members help each other as well as being helped. Often led by another caregiver, the group offers each participant an opportunity to reach out and support others.

Psychoeducational groups help caregivers who are experiencing stressful caregiving problems. These problems are often exacerbated by other long standing issues. For example, the stress being experienced by a daughter caring for her mother may be increased by feelings that the lack of help received from another sister stems from past disputes over other issues. Psychoeducational groups can help by: (a) increasing caregivers' understanding of the relative for whom they are caring and the disease processes involved; (b) helping spouses and other caregivers to make better use of family, friends and other supports; (c) enabling caregivers to consider alternative approaches to dealing with the stresses they are experiencing; (d) encouraging caregivers to take better care of themselves and to balance the needs of the care recipient with their own needs; (e) addressing problematic relationships with the care recipient or other family members; and (f) improving caregivers' skills in responding to ADL and IADL needs (McCallion, Toseland, and Diehl, 1994). These groups are usually led by a professional leader.

Social, recreational and educational groups offer caregivers social contact, recreation, and fun. Gardening clubs are a good example of this type of group. Although their goal is primarily recreational or informational, these groups also maintain and enhance caregivers' abilities, and improve their self-esteem. Such groups help caregivers because they offer support in a setting removed from caregiving. The members' common interest in the group's social, recreational, or educational activity and the experiences they share as a result of engaging in it, form the bond among them. In general, program activities include: discussion of current events; reminiscence and life review; educational topics; aerobic and other physical exercise; dance, theater, and other expressive activities; special events; and table games (Toseland, 1995). Leaders of such groups usually have activity-related skills.

Support groups in all three categories address the problems of isolation which many caregivers experience by bringing these caregivers into contact with others. Therefore, they are an important resource for caregiving families. Many professionals such as physicians, nurses, social workers, psychologists, speech therapists, horticulture therapists, and activities staff come in contact with caregiving families through doctors' offices, short-term hospitalizations, referrals, visiting health services, respite and day programs. These professionals are an important source of information about such supportive group programs and often facilitate caregivers locating and joining a suitable program (see McCallion, Diehl, & Toseland, 1994, for a fuller description of the roles professionals play in connecting caregivers to supportive groups).

However, attendance at groups requires that the caregiver be able to leave the care recipient alone for a period of time. In situations where a lot of physical caregiving is required (for example, for persons in the terminal stages of cancer or who have experienced debilitating strokes) or where safety issues require constant supervision (for example, some persons with Alzheimer's disease), the very social isolation that groups are intended to alleviate may mean that there is no one available or trusted who can take over the caregiving role so the caregiver can attend the group. Some caregivers simply will not entrust care to others. Also, as in the case of the spouse caregiver previously mentioned, many caregivers wish to involve the care recipient in the same activities.

An additional concern is that many groups only meet for short periods.

One husband caring for a wife with Alzheimer's disease said that he really enjoyed attending the public affairs discussion group held once a week at his public library, but when the group stopped meeting for the summer, he felt even more isolated and alone. When the group formed again in the fall, he decided not to attend. For these families there is a need for activities that caregivers will find enjoyable; involve both caregiver and care recipient; can easily occur inside the home as well as outside the home; can engage the caregiver's interest and can be maintained as an activity over a long period of time; and validate that it is appropriate for caregivers to occasionally take care of their own needs. Such activities should also have the potential to encourage caregivers to contemplate taking advantage of group activities outside of the home. Such a program is the Caregiver Horticulture Program.

CAREGIVER HORTICULTURE PROGRAM

The Caregiver Horticulture Program (CHP) draws from the rich tradition of horticultural therapy. Horticultural therapy utilizes gardening, plants, floral materials, and vegetation to stimulate an individual's interest, and to develop leisure and vocational skills (Morgan, 1989; Moore, 1989). Although much of the evidence is anecdotal rather than systematically derived, for a variety of populations plants have been found to assist post-surgical recovery, to reduce use of pain medications, and to increase positive behaviors and affect (Sneh & Tristan, 1991; Williams, 1989; Ulrick, 1984). Horticultural therapy activities also have the advantages of being low cost, able to use materials within the home, and able to build upon participants' existing interests and skills.

Horticultural therapy activities are best delivered by a trained horticultural therapist. However, CHP draws upon established materials and ideas developed by certified horticultural therapists so that it may be implemented by other professionals visiting the family. It should be noted that the American Horticultural Therapy Association (AHTA) maintains a registry of certified individuals who may be contacted about delivering a program like CHP, or who may be willing to provide consultation to other professionals considering undertaking this program. One example of professionals cooperating in this manner is a hospital-based horticultural therapist who designed a CHP intervention that a visiting health nurse implemented, with the horticultural therapist providing telephone consultation to the nurse and to the caregiving family. Delivery of CHP by a variety of professionals does mean that monitoring of the program can be combined with other professional visits. This approach adds to CHP's cost-effectiveness and increases the likelihood that families will consider CHP because it will be introduced and monitored by individuals with whom the family already has a relationship.

CHP is a two-phase program. In the initial start-up phase a needs assessment for the caregiver and the care recipient and an inventory of the environment are conducted. The assessment addresses three areas:

1. What kinds of gardening activities are currently enjoyed and have been enjoyed in the past by the caregiver and care recipient? Examples must include caring for indoor plants, or growing herbs, vegetables or flowers outside.
2. How functional is the home for beginning and maintaining horticulture activities? Issues to consider are the amount of light and space, availability of indoor and outdoor areas to develop year-round plant activities, ability to regulate temperatures and to maintain irrigation, and storage space for equipment.
3. To what extent can the care recipient participate? For some care recipients, participation includes actually cultivating plants and may require the development of modified planting beds for wheelchair and bedside access. For other families, participation may mean the care recipient being able to watch and communicate with the caregiver while the caregiver is engaged in horticulture activities.

Upon completion of this assessment, three to four short- and long-term activities are then introduced as part of the start-up phase. Separate activities should be selected so the caregiver or caregiver and care recipient can identify tasks to work on at least 2-3 times per week. The therapist should be cautious of recommending too many activities lest the program becomes very expensive for the family, or require them to commit more time than they have available. Good resources for identifying short and long-term activities are the activity descriptions in *Growing with Gardening* (Moore, 1989) and *Growing Together* (Morgan, 1989). The therapist listens to the caregiver and care recipient and helps them select specific activities that they are interested in implementing. Activities that build upon existing caregiver and care recipient knowledge and interest offer the greatest likelihood of success. However, the therapist does not discourage the caregiver and care recipient from trying something new. The therapist's advice on new activities relates to their feasibility, given the space and other physical constraints of the home, and how activities might be modified in response.

Making leaf wreaths, forcing flower bulbs, preparing seed tapes, drying flowers, and rooting cuttings are all short-term activities which can be accomplished in the home, can occur outside normal growing seasons, and lend themselves to either independent activities for the caregiver or to being broken down into smaller activities in which the care recipient can also participate. Drawing upon the ideas found in Moore (1989) and Morgan (1989), the therapist also encourages the caregiver and care recipient to think about additional activities that build upon these initial efforts. For example, early spring seed tapes can become late spring outdoor flower and vegetable plantings; dried flowers from an initial project can be scented and cured for use as potpourri; and rooted cuttings can become plants that the caregiver and care recipient include in a terrarium they work on together.

Longer-term projects are also considered and selected in this phase. Some long-term activities combine a number of short-term activities. The therapist works with some families on growing herbs indoors. Growing scented herbs such as lemon balm and mint provides visual and olfactory stimulation for both caregiver and care recipient over time. The therapist also discusses with the caregiver and care recipient how they may later use the herbs in other related activities including cooking or for making potpourri. Other families may feel stymied by a lack of space, or because the care recipient's new limitations prevent her/him from coming outside to the garden to help or even to watch the caregiver. Here, in a long-term project, the therapist shares information on developing container and window box gardens which can then be worked on or viewed from wheelchairs or even from bed, or on approaches such as square foot gardening which make maximum use of small spaces. The therapist then encourages the caregiver and care recipient to use winter months effectively to plan for their garden, helping them to identify vegetables or flowers that can be seeded and started indoors, and identifying needed materials. The therapist also suggests gardening books and magazines that they may subscribe to or borrow from their library, and identifies related television programs the caregiver and care recipient may watch together.

After the caregiver or the caregiver and the care recipient have selected several short-term and long-term activities as part of their individual CHP plan, the therapist helps them write up their plan. In that plan, they identify the necessary supplies, the steps involved in carrying out the activities, and a timeline for implementing the project. The therapist also helps locate supplies that may already be in the home, and provides information and other assistance on placing orders or picking up other supplies.

For some families with well developed horticulture skills and good existing gardening and horticulture resources, all of these steps can be completed in one or two visits. Other families will require more active support from the therapist. Some of this support can be provided through periodic telephone calls. It is also a good idea to give caregivers telephone numbers for the local cooperative extension office, volunteer master gardeners, gardening clubs, and local commercial greenhouses who are willing to offer free telephone advice on horticulture-related issues. All families, however, also benefit from periodic follow-ups from the therapist.

The follow-up phase usually involves a minimum of two telephone or in-person contacts with the caregiver. This is a good opportunity to make use of the expertise of a consultant horticultural therapist if the professional offering CHP is not one her/himself. A conference call is sometimes appropriate for one or both of the follow-up contacts involving the caregiver, the professional offering CHP and the horticultural therapy consultant. The first follow-up usually occurs one month after the individual CHP plan has been established. The therapist's prime focus is problem-solving. Often caregivers and care recipients are very enthusiastic at the time the plan is developed. This enthusiasm does not always translate into action and the one month follow-up is often very helpful in answering remaining or new questions, identifying solutions to problems that have arisen, and reenergizing their efforts. Some caregivers and care recipients may say they have changed their minds about participating. The therapist should respect this, although occasionally a little probing reveals relatively minor barriers have obstructed caregivers and care recipients, and with a little assistance they will recommit themselves to the program.

It is recommended that the second follow-up contact occur at the next major change of season. This is a time when activities change and caregivers and care recipients may have new questions. Also, if participation in activities has begun to wane, it is a good opportunity to re-examine the plan, look for ways to improve the plan, or perhaps begin anew. Therapists will also find that the change of season is a culminating event for activities that caregivers and care recipients have undertaken to this point. Seedlings that were nurtured will now be planted; plants that were tended may now yield their fruit. Therefore, this end of season contact is also an important opportunity for the therapist to congratulate the caregiver and care recipient on what they have achieved. Finally, some caregivers and care recipients, as they have begun to enjoy these activities, may welcome advice now on how to further refine their CHP plan. Caregivers may also be more ready to consider participating occasionally in horticulture and garden-related projects or groups outside of the home. The follow-up contact is an important opportunity to assist them in locating and beginning to attend such a group.

First Case Example

Mrs. Brown, a 70-year-old woman caring at home for her 74-year-old husband was referred to the visiting psychiatric nurse. Home health care services were already being provided to assist with personal care for Mr. Brown, who had experienced a stroke which left him paralyzed on the right side. However, staff reported that Mrs. Brown seemed very depressed, and did not appear to be eating well or taking care of herself, and this was starting to impact on her ability to care for her husband. The psychiatric nurse found Mrs. Brown was feeling very overwhelmed by all the disruptions created in their lives by her husband's stroke and the related care created in their lives. Not least among these was the isolation she now felt. Her husband had been the only driver in the family, and all the activities they had taken part in were some distance away. Also, although her daughter was willing to take care of Mr. Brown occasionally so that Mrs. Brown could go out on her own, Mrs. Brown "didn't feel right about it" because her daughter was already taking care of two small children.

As the psychiatric nurse and Mrs. Brown talked, it became clear that what would alleviate some of Mrs. Brown's sense of being overwhelmed would be a return of some order, and control in her life, and "having something to look forward to, and something to do together that isn't about strokes." The psychiatric nurse talked to Mrs. Brown about how some of the care tasks might be better structured to provide order and give her more control of her time. She then asked Mrs. Brown about activities in which she and Mr. Brown had engaged in the past. Mrs. Brown mentioned that every year her husband had grown vegetables in their garden, and that she had developed and maintained a number of flower beds, but that all of that had been abandoned. The psychiatric nurse, who was also a trained horticulture therapist, pointed out to Mrs. Brown the benefits many people gain from cultivating and maintaining plants and suggested there might be ways to reconnect with past gardening activities. She suggested some activities to consider and left a copy of Moore's book for Mrs. Brown to look at.

On her next visit the psychiatric nurse found that both Mr. and Mrs. Brown had looked at the book and found some things that they wanted to do. Their daughter had given them some cuttings and they had started some indoor plants. Mr. Brown wished they could have a vegetable garden again. Mrs. Brown felt it was just too much work. The psychiatric nurse shared some materials on square foot gardening and pointed out that there was a small area close to the kitchen window that could be easily cultivated and that Mr. Brown could see. They discussed activities Mr. Brown could help with and checked the listings of their PBS station for a television program dedicated to square foot gardening. Mrs. Brown was still skeptical and the nurse warned against taking on a project that was too large. However, the Browns decided they would develop a small garden.

The psychiatric nurse was not scheduled to visit the Browns again, so she followed up by telephone. They had decided to go ahead with the garden. Saturday afternoons were now their garden planning time, since that was when the related program was on television. Also, their daughter had borrowed some gardening books from the library, and Mr. Brown, with some assistance, had begun making seed tapes. The nurse called again when planting season was about to begin. Mrs. Brown said they were getting started and both she and her husband were really enjoying the activities: "In some ways, doing things together like this is like old times. Some days are still tough, but I just grab a bag of potting soil and repot some plants and by the end I feel more relaxed, things aren't as overwhelming." Her son-in-law rented a rototiller and prepared the area for the garden.

Mrs. Brown also told the nurse she had gone for the afternoon to a local flower show. "I felt really guilty about going, but it was nice to be out of the house . . . and Bill (her husband) wanted me to go. I got all sorts of brochures and samples that I brought back for him and I told him all about it. It wasn't like he was there himself, but I tried to make him feel that . . . I got some information on a local gardening club . . . They seemed like very nice people . . . I don't know if I'll go . . . They meet once a week . . . I'll talk to Bill and I'll talk to my daughter."

Second Case Example

Mrs. Jones had been caring for her mother for three years. Her mother's Alzheimer's Disease had reached a stage at which she required constant supervision. Mrs. Jones had left her job to dedicate herself to her mother's care. Her husband and her own children tried to help. However, both children were now in college, and her husband traveled a lot with his job—a job, as Mrs. Jones put it, on which they all depended. The local chapter of the Alzheimer's Association had initiated a telephone support program using volunteers who agreed to contact homebound caregivers of persons with Alzheimer's Disease. A paid professional on the Association staff provided training and consultation for the volunteers. Mrs. Lucas was the volunteer keeping in touch with Mrs. Jones. After a number of telephone calls it became clear that Mrs. Jones was reluctant to allow anyone else to care for her mother—not even so that she, herself, might get a break. Yet she said that she would love to get a break, once in a while, just to do something for herself.

Mrs. Jones indicated that the biggest problem was it was difficult to predict when her mother would have a good day, or when she might decide to take a nap. What Mrs. Jones said she needed was something she could turn to and do for herself at a moment's notice, and at the same time, something from which she could walk away easily if her mother needed her. Mrs. Lucas recalled that as part of her orientation to the volunteer program a number of activities that might be useful for family caregivers and for persons with Alzheimer's Disease had been described. This part of the training had included a short workshop by a horticultural therapist on easily developed seasonal and year-round activities using plants. Mrs. Lucas asked Mrs. Jones if she had any interest in caring for plants. Mrs. Jones indicated she had enjoyed plants in the past, and she still had a couple of hanging baskets in her kitchen. However, she had really not worked with plants since her mother moved in. Mrs. Lucas explained the workshop she had attended and asked Mrs. Jones if she could send her some information. Mrs. Jones said that would be fine.

Mrs. Lucas then contacted her supervisor and explained what she had discussed with Mrs. Jones. They agreed that horticultural activities might be very helpful for Mrs. Jones, and reviewed the packet of materials they had received as part of the horticultural therapy workshop to identify activities that they might recommend. They pulled out materials on hanging baskets and on growing herbs indoors. They also contacted the horticultural therapist who had led the workshop. She pointed out that if the intervention was going to be successful, it was important to offer Mrs. Jones a number of different activities, from which to choose and to offer opportunities for year-round activities. She recommended that they begin with the hanging baskets and herbs, but also encouraged Mrs. Jones to consider holiday-related activities such as making wreaths during the winter months.

Mrs. Lucas mailed information on the benefits of horticultural therapy and guidelines for two horticultural activities to Mrs. Jones. Over the next few weeks they discussed Mrs. Jones' efforts to begin these activities and to fit them into her schedule. Mrs. Jones immediately repotted the two hanging baskets she already had and planted some herbs in window boxes. However, she complained that she only had so many windows in which to hang baskets, and she could only look so often at the herbs to see if they were coming up. As the horticultural therapist had suggested, Mrs. Lucas then talked to Mrs. Jones about starting some seasonal crafts activities. Mrs. Jones was reluctant, but she had her husband pick up a form and some materials for a wreath from a crafts store. During her next telephone call, Mrs. Jones told Mrs. Lucas that the previous night her mother got out of bed repeatedly so that she herself ended up sitting up all night waiting to redirect her mother. At about 3 a.m. she noticed the wreath materials sitting in the kitchen, and since she was not going to get any sleep anyway, started working with them. She told Mrs. Lucas that she did not do a very good job because she was just too tired, but it helped her get through the night and distracted her from worrying about her mother. Now she planned to take apart what she had done and to restart the wreath the next time she got a few minutes to herself. A few weeks later she reported that the wreath was finished and that it was the first thing she had done just for herself in years. Mrs. Jones asked Mrs. Lucas for information on other activities she could undertake in this way at home.

Mrs. Lucas, herself, was becoming more interested in plants, gardening, and related activities through her discussions with Mrs. Jones. She took some books out from the library on the subject and attended related workshops. In the months that followed, when Mrs. Jones' mother's condition continued to worsen, Mrs. Lucas would offer Mrs. Jones encouragement to continue working with her plants and suggestions about how to find time and materials for activities. She would also stress the importance of Mrs. Jones making time for herself through these activities. Mrs. Jones continued to report how helpful she found these activities.

CONCLUSION

Horticultural therapy activities offer an additional dimension to the range of services available to family caregivers. They involve both the caregiver and care recipient, can be adapted to any home situation, and may help isolated caregivers become comfortable with doing things outside the home. Other professionals should also feel encouraged to use horticultural therapists as consultants and to obtain additional information and perhaps subsequent training in this area.

REFERENCES

Gevalnik, J.M., & Simonsick, E.M. (1993). Physical disability in older Americans. *The Journals of Gerontology, 48*(Special Issue), 3-10.

Lawton, M.P., Kleban, M.H., Moss, M., Rovine, M., & Glicksman, A. (1989). Measuring caregiver appraisal. *Journal of Gerontology, 44,* 61-71.

McCallion, P., Diehl, M., & Toseland, R. (1994). Support group interventions for family caregivers of Alzheimer's Disease patients. *Seminars in Speech and Language, 15,* 257-270.

McCallion, P., Toseland, R.W., & Diehl, M. (1994). Social work practice with caregivers of frail older adults. *Research in Social Work Practice, 4,* 64-88.

Moore, B. (1989). *Growing with gardening.* Charlotte, NC: North Carolina Botanical Gardens.

Morgan, B. (1989). *Growing together.* Pittsburgh, PA: Pittsburgh Civic Garden Center.

Sneh, N. & Tristan, J. (1991). Plant material arrangements in therapy. *Journal of Therapeutic Horticulture, 6,* 16-20.

Stone, R. Cafferta, G.S., & Sangl, J. (1987). Caregivers of the frail elderly: A national profile. *The Gerontologist, 27,* 616-626.

Stone, R.I., & Kemper, P. (1989). Spouses and children of disabled elders: How large a constituency for long-term care reform. *The Milbank Quarterly, 64,* 485-506.

Toseland, R.W. (1995). *Group Work with Older Adults and Family Caregivers.* 2nd Edition. New York: Springer.

Toseland, R., Smith, G.C., & McCallion, P. (1995). Supporting the "family" in family caregiving. In G. Smith, S.S. Tobin, B.A. Robertson-Tchabo, & P. Power (Eds.), *Enabling Aging Families: Directions for practice and policy.* Newbury Park, CA: Sage.

Williams, S. (1989). Evaluation of a horticulture therapy program in a short-term psychiatric ward. *Journal of Therapeutic Horticulture, 4,* 29-38.

Ulrick, R. (1984). View through their window may influence recovery from surgery. *Science, 221,* 420.

Zarit, S.H., Orr, N.K., & Zarit, J.M. (1985). *The hidden victims of Alzheimer's disease: Families under stress.* New York: New York University Press.

Horticultural Therapy in Residential Long-Term Care: Applications from Research on Health, Aging, and Institutional Life

Louise K. Stein

SUMMARY. A sociocultural conceptual framework for the work of horticultural therapists provides a foundation for more effective and compassionate gardening programs for long-term care residents. Contemporary American health care emphasizes technical, biomedical approaches to most problems related to aging, chronic illness and frailty. However, evidence from qualitative research, personal narratives about life in a nursing home and observations from the author's work in a resident-centered nursing home gardening program illustrate the benefits of a sociocultural conceptual framework in therapeutic practice. *[Article copies available for a fee from The Haworth Document Delivery Service: 1-800-342-9678. E-mail address: getinfo@haworth.com]*

A color snapshot depicts two women, both white-haired and smiling, looking forward over large pots of full-blooming red, yellow and peach

---

Louise K. Stein, PhD, is Clinical Assistant Professor, SUNY HSC Syracuse, Clinical Campus, Binghamton, NY.

Address correspondence to: Louise K. Stein, PhD, 56 Centennial Avenue, Brockport, NY 14420.

[Haworth co-indexing entry note]: "Horticultural Therapy in Residential Long-Term Care: Applications from Research on Health, Aging, and Institutional Life." Stein, Louise K. Co-published simultaneously in *Activities, Adaptation & Aging* (The Haworth Press, Inc.) Vol. 22, No. 1/2, 1997, pp. 107-124; and: *Horticultural Therapy and the Older Adult Population* (ed: Suzanne E. Wells) The Haworth Press, Inc., 1997, pp. 107-124. Single or multiple copies of this article are available for a fee from The Haworth Document Delivery Service [1-800-342-9678, 9:00 a.m. - 5:00 p.m. (EST). E-mail address: getinfo@haworth.com].

tulips. One of the women is in a wheelchair, the other is standing, supported by a walker. What strikes the viewer about the women in this photo are their warm, self-assured gazes outward beyond the colorful tulips on the table next to them.

The two women in the photograph are nursing home residents. They planted the tulips as a fall gardening project done by themselves and other residents in their nursing home. Now, after a few months of cold storage, the tulips were blooming in the dayroom, a multipurpose common room, of their nursing home unit. The photograph was taken by a member of one of the women's family. I was given a copy of the photo by both of the women as a gift to show their pride in this colorful show and to express appreciation for my contribution to the display.

My observations on the role of resident-centered gardening in institutional settings are based on five years of experience as coordinator and participant in a horticultural therapy program for older adults in upstate New York. I developed and managed a year-round gardening program for older adults who live in a residential community which I shall call Riverview. Riverview includes congregate apartments, an adult care facility, a home care agency and a nursing home. In this paper, the case study of the Riverview Horticulture Program is based primarily on my experience in the 150-resident nursing home. The theoretical framework discussed here stems from my training as a medical anthropologist and from nine years as full-time faculty member and gerontologist in the Geriatric Medicine program of a medical college.

The purpose of this paper is to propose a sociocultural conceptual framework for the work of horticultural therapists, as well as other rehabilitation and recreation therapists, who work in long-term care institutions. In this paper I will:

1. Introduce theories about, and findings on, the organization of health care and institutional life;
2. Suggest ways in which therapists might interpret their work in institutional settings; and
3. Describe some of the ways a horticultural therapy program based on this framework benefits residents in a nursing home.

I will introduce six concepts through a selected review of literature on health policy, aging and the qualitative study of nursing home life. These concepts are: the biomedicalization of aging; total institutions and the medical model of care; social interpretations of resident behavior; individual choice in a nursing home; memory and lived experience in a nursing home; and poverty and nursing home life. In these discussions, I will incorporate case study examples from my observations in the Riverview nursing home gardening program. Finally, I will conclude with an overview of the benefits to residents by returning to the description of the photograph which begins this paper.

Why is a sociocultural conceptual framework important to the work of a therapist working in a residential institution—in this case a nursing home? A conceptual framework is important in order to place observations and understandings about one's work in an institution within a body of knowledge which goes beyond the everyday tasks of therapeutic work. A sociocultural conceptual framework can help a therapist in a nursing home, for example, to analyze what might otherwise be disparaged as anecdotal information. This conceptual base may help a therapist better understand a resident's actions, which in turn can influence the therapist's treatment choices. These choices can run the gamut from the manner in which a therapist decides to approach a resident and family member, to the therapist's rationale for resident advocacy, to the way the therapist's role is actuated in the larger institution.

THE BIOMEDICALIZATION OF AGING

The way in which most Americans, including health professionals, think about aging and the processes and problems involved in aging has changed significantly in this century. Now, most aging issues are thought of in medical or biomedical terms. This shift in thinking and in practice is called the biomedicalization of aging. The biomedicalization of aging has two aspects: (a) thinking about aging as a medical problem with a focus on diseases, their cause, treatment and management as the best approach to the challenges of getting old; and (b) practice in all areas related to aging is medically oriented because practitioners think of aging as a medical problem (Estes and Binney, 1989). With increasing frequency, aging is defined as a medical problem, with the basic social and behavioral processes of aging seen as secondary or redefined in purely clinical medical terms. The medical model influences every aspect of aging, most especially all types of therapies, as well as "research policy making, and the way we think about aging and even science, as it is defined and evaluated in terms of a biomedical structure of thought . . . " (Estes and Binney, 1989: 588). This occurs despite the mounting evidence that social and behavioral variables are major factors in explaining health in aging.

Understanding basic tenets of the biomedicalization of aging is important to practitioners in nursing homes for two reasons.

1. Like medical practice in which the focus is on the individual and the disease, the process of biomedicalization reduces complex health issues that may involve interrelationships among systems to be dealt with as one individual's problems. This individualization may be beneficial in the relationship between doctor and patient. "However, it limits the consideration of larger social and environmental factors, because the primary focus is on illness as an individual problem with individual causes and individual solutions" (Estes and Binney, 1989: 588).

2. The biomedical model rests on technological solutions in treatment. This model directly contradicts the "coping strategies" important to the majority of older persons who deal with multiple chronic illnesses.

Nursing home staff members are very familiar with the social foundations of their work. They know a purely medical solution to the problems of their residents, no matter how many or how serious their illnesses, does not exist. The residents live in a complex array of relationships and expectations within the nursing home. In addition, some residents are still very involved in family relationships which brings another level of complexity to life in the institution. Often the more social the approach, the more successful the nursing home is in terms of both resident and staff satisfaction.

One distinctly social model approach to nursing home life is the Eden Alternative (Thomas, 1994). This nonmedical model approach to nursing home care was developed by a physician with experience as a nursing home medical director. Although residents have excellent medical and nursing care, the mission of a nursing home adopting the Eden Alternative approach is to create a "human habitat" within which residents live. This habitat incorporates the nurturing of plants, animals and children in the model of care. The Eden Alternative is not just a social model of nursing home care; it is designed as a new type of nursing home culture which would be an antidote to the austerity and morbid outcomes of the "total institution."

TOTAL INSTITUTIONS AND THE MEDICAL MODEL OF CARE

The two women in the photograph described at the beginning of this paper are nursing home residents. They are sitting in the dayroom of their nursing home unit. "Dayroom" is an unusual term when describing the interior space of a home in American culture. In Rybczynski's (1986) discussion of common rooms in a home, there is no mention of a dayroom. Depending on the wealth of the owner and the historical period, a common room might be called a parlor, sitting room, drawing room, living room, family room, dining room and so on, but not a dayroom. I have only heard the word "dayroom" used as a term to denote a common room in an institutional setting. The use of a special vocabulary is one of the characteristics of an institutional culture. More important, nursing homes, as a type of institution, have a prescribed set of rules or norms: a complicated system of understandings, beliefs and expectations of which all of its inhabitants, including residents and staff, are a part.

An important theoretical elaboration of the social and cultural definition of institutional life is that of Erving Goffman (1961). This work rests on the central concept of the total institution as "a place of residence and work where a large number of like-situated individuals, cut off from the wider society for an appreciable period of time, together lead an enclosed, formally administered round of life" (p. xiii). There are many types of institutions which share the characteristics of total institutions, among them mental hospitals, prisons, boarding schools, monasteries and nursing homes.

Much has been written in reaction to this understanding of the social organization of nursing homes and other types of residential facilities for older people (Baldwin, Harris and Kelly, 1993). In practice, a physician colleague was repulsed by my use of the concept of "total institution" in teaching medical students about the nature of life in nursing homes. As a medical practitioner, he saw nursing homes as warm, clean places for older incapacitated people to live, places that provided nourishment and activities to keep residents occupied and socially involved. I argued that all of those seemingly positive attributes aside, how was one to understand the feelings and behaviors of residents and of staff which did not coincide with this benevolent and ahistorical understanding of the function of nursing homes?

The concept of "total institution" and the characteristics of social organization and corresponding attributes of staff and residents allows any practitioner working in a nursing home to put their own behavior and feelings and those of others living and working there into a broader framework. The lack of privacy, loss of status, restrictions on autonomy and controls on almost every facet of daily life have negative consequences for residents who tend to feel weak, inferior and dependent.

One of the men in our gardening group exemplified these resident attributes. Stan had lived in the nursing home for a number of months when I invited him to join our regular group gardening sessions. I had visited his unit and noticed all the well tended plants on the window shelf in the dayroom, and was told Stan was the caretaker of the plants. The first time we spoke, and for the many times we spoke over the next few years, Stan rarely looked directly at me, but always with a tilted head and a very deferential manner. Once he called himself an "inmate" in the nursing home. Stan was a very well oriented and capable person and very adept at getting around the home in his wheelchair. I asked him if he would water geranium cuttings and annual seedlings at times other than group meetings. Stan agreed to do the watering because he loved working with plants. Yet, if he needed the assistance of any staff person to accomplish this task, Stan would not do it. For example, if our plants were temporarily moved, Stan would not ask their new location. When I asked him why he did not ask, he indicated he did not want to do anything that might call attention to himself and lead to blame. This occurred in a very good nursing home, one in which scolding or mean spirited exchanges with residents by staff were highly unusual.

Feeling blameworthy and stigmatized are normal feelings for residents in American nursing homes. The link between the "poor house" of nineteenth century America and today's nursing home is a direct one—the County Home where, earlier in this century the destitute infirm could find refuge in old age (see Vladeck, 1980, for an incisive history of nursing homes and public policy). For example, in the upstate New York county in which I have made most of these observations, the County Almshouse became the County Infirmary which eventually metamorphosed into the largest nursing home in the county. Many 80- and 90-year-old residents in nursing homes today are very aware of this history, even when they do not reside in a "county" or public nursing home. As one Riverview resident sadly said to me, "I never thought I'd live in the Poor House." Nursing home residents may feel that no matter how comfortable the accommodations, or how kindly the staff treats them, by virtue of their residing in an institution in old age, they are "eating the crust of humility" and as a result feel stigmatized.

Critics of nursing homes often name the use of a medical model for resident care as a central problem. This model developed in hospitals in which patients need treatment for diseases of an acute nature. Disease diagnosis and treatment, often technologically based, are organized within a hierarchical system in which physicians are key. Generally speaking, few nursing homes are organized on a specifically medical model; however, as resident populations become older and sicker, administrators, medical directors and even family members turn to medical interpretations of a resident's situation to find answers to very complex life problems.

Often the environment adds to the medicalization of nursing home care. Many nursing homes look like small hospitals. Rooms are arranged on either side of a long corridor, and the focus of a unit is often a large nursing desk where resident charts are kept, medications are locked, and the major nursing/medical communication work on the unit occurs. There have been numerous discussions about transformations in this basic design, notably the work of Koncelik (1976), Cohen and Day (1993), Calkins (1988), Hoglund (1985), and Regnier (1994), to name just a few of the leaders in the field of housing and institutional design for older people. Even with innovative design in the United States and Europe, most nursing homes today are close approximations of the basic double-loaded corridor design, which is an offshoot of the hospital environment in which nurses, allied health professionals and physicians are trained. The influence of the acute model of care cannot help but affect the way in which residents, often called patients, are cared for in nursing homes.

Yet another environmental dimension, the larger health care environment, is increasingly important. Specifically, many hospitals have vertically integrated such long-term care systems as nursing homes, home care, assisted living, and elder apartment housing under the hospital system umbrella. From the patient's point of view, this integration may help to provide for greater continuity in care, but it can also mean that an acute care model and medical approach may persist into the long-term, chronic care institution.

SOCIAL INTERPRETATIONS OF RESIDENT BEHAVIOR

Why is a socially oriented model of care so important in the nursing home environment? The best evidence comes from the descriptions of nursing home life from sociologists and anthropologists, and from residents themselves. In the following paragraphs I will provide a few descriptions of nursing home life which contain insights that apply to the work of horticultural therapists and recreation specialists in these settings.

Living and Dying at Murray Manor (Gubrium, 1975) is now a classic in terms of qualitative analysis of resident care in a nursing home. The analysis is replete with transcriptions of staff meetings, as well as discussions among the researcher, staff and residents and among residents themselves. For anyone who works in a nursing home these transcriptions will be identical to ones you may have heard recently in the home. Gubrium's critique of the psychologistic approach to resident care is particularly incisive.

> To top staff (N.B.: Top staff includes the administrator, medical director, nursing director, social worker, activity director, occupational and physical therapists, dietician or other nonfloor staff), good clientele care is care that is individually oriented. This means that the needs of the patient or resident are believed to come before institutional expedients. If a choice must be made between a care policy that will hinder the least able patient's well-being and having no policy at all, top staff considers it best to opt for no policy (p. 44) . . . When top staff seeks an explanation for a problematic client's behavior, it searches that person's individual background. If that doesn't suggest an answer, his "typical" personality is considered. Top staff overestimate the unity of personality to the detriment of considering social explanations of human behavior (p. 45) . . . Rarely does top staff seek social explanations for clientele behavior. It believes that people do things because of their personal desires or "quirks." Although top staff often casually recount the interaction between persons that led to the particular actions of a patient or resident, such interaction is not given serious attention as an official explanation of behavior. The official causes of clientele behavior lie within the persons themselves, not in the circumstances of their everyday lives in or out of the Manor. (p. 46)

Staff will suggest psychological explanations, to the exclusion of social ones, of the individual behavior of anyone living or working in the nursing home. For example, our gardening group often had one activity assistant assigned to work along with gardening volunteers and residents. A new activity assistant, Meg, began working with our group on the day we began planting outdoors. I noticed she had not actually "dug in" at any point in our session and so I encouraged her to participate by planting a few annuals with us. She replied sweetly, "Oh, I don't like to get my hands dirty. I'm happy to just watch all of you." After the session, I met with the activity director and suggested that although Meg was a very agreeable person, I did not think she was an appropriate choice to assist with the gardening program because she refused to put her hands in soil. The director immediately consoled me by saying this was a "personality conflict" between me and the assistant, but given time, we would get along just fine. I was taken aback. I insisted this situation was about the need for

someone who could give hands-on assistance to resident gardeners in the
gardening program. My view was not heard.

INDIVIDUAL CHOICE IN A NURSING HOME

Each weekly gardening session at Riverview includes 10 to 12 resident
gardeners, all in wheelchairs. Most suffer multiple sensory and mobility
losses, such as vision or hearing loss and the use of only one arm, as well
as other health problems. Because the main goals of the program are to
have residents themselves do as much of the gardening as possible and to
provide warm social interactions throughout each session, the program has
a group of adult volunteers as helpers. Five experienced gardeners have
chosen to work in the program as volunteers because they are interested in
providing a stimulating social environment for nursing home residents.
The volunteers assist the resident gardeners who ask for help to accomplish a task, and keep up a stream of friendly and supportive discussion
with residents throughout each session. The gardening program is fun and
productive for the residents because of the physical activity, the resultant
beautiful plants and the companionable relationships which develop between the volunteers and the residents.

The Ends of Time: Life and Work in a Nursing Home (Savishinsky,
1991) is particularly interesting to therapists who work with volunteers in
their programs. The book starts with an anthropologist's account of the
development of a pet therapy program, and expands to examine how
employees coped with their demanding jobs, along with brief and poignant
biographies of some of the residents with an emphasis on their lives as
older people living in Elmwood Grove. A long analysis devoted to the
volunteers in the program examines their role in the pet program, in the
lives of the residents and in the larger institution. In the chapter "Altruism
and Aging," Savishinsky analyzes volunteering in general: how the experience in the nursing home affected the volunteers; why some continued to
choose to volunteer and others stopped; and suggestions to improve the
volunteer experience both for volunteers and for the institution.

The Riverside gardening program has as an overarching philosophy–
choice in participation is important. Volunteers choose to be regular assistants at sessions and nursing home residents are asked if they wish to
attend each session. The group of gardening residents would be recogniz-
able to anyone familiar with nursing home populations. There is one
difference between this group and a random sample of the Riverview
nursing home population; the gardening program does not usually have
demented residents as participants. Yet because our program has existed

for more than five years, there are residents in the program who have progressively shown more symptoms of dementia. These residents continue in the program until they are no longer able to make the choice to attend. The gardening program always functions with the explicit understanding that residents are asked to make a choice about whether they wish to attend or not. The gardening session is a regular part of the activities calendar, but regular participants are not automatically wheeled to the sessions. Residents are invited to attend. It is a choice that each participant is asked to make:

> The idea of independence is central to the American character and ethos . . . While choice represents the social or meaningful environment in which independence exists, choice also may be culturally viewed as independence operationalized . . . The environment of independence–the ability to make choices–is closely linked to the idea of control. Most clearly, people make choices about that over which they have control or in order to gain control . . . Choice making is diagnostic of personhood in American culture. People lose their sense of being and integrity as individuals when they are no longer able to choose for themselves (p. 3). In American culture, freedom is said to be found in wide-open spaces, through individual agency, and in the broad choices about living life that people must make. For older people, the big picture has often been painted in. Yet by the means of the miracle of symbolic process, freedom to make choices about one's daily life–viewed on the broadest scale–can also be operationalized through small-scale decision-making in the home, even ranged around issues of health-based restriction . . . (p. 145) (Rubinstein et al., 1992)

Rubenstein and his colleagues developed these insights about the importance of independence and choice in the lives of older people in research on frail older people who lived on their own in the community. I believe the ideas on personhood and choice apply equally to older Americans who are capable of such choice, but who live in an institution which puts uncompromising limits on choice making. The gardening program leaders at Riverview ask participants to exercise their prerogatives before each session and decide if they wish to join the group. Whether affirmative or not, residents' decisions are always respected.

MEMORY AND LIVED EXPERIENCE IN A NURSING HOME

For those who work in nursing homes, the term "memory" is usually linked with negative states. Loss of memory, impairment in short-term memory and confused memory are pervasive phrases in nursing home vocabulary when referring to residents' cognitive function. Rarely is there an understanding that for some residents, the building of new memories might occur in a nursing home.

Limbo (1979) is an autobiographical account of life in a nursing home by Carobeth Laird and is particularly interesting in terms of the type and nature of the memories she collected. This is a direct and nonanalytical account of her days as a resident in a home in Arizona. In one of the few sections in the book in which Laird describes her nursing home experience as satisfying, she describes the impact of moving to a bed by the window. The following are excerpts from a three-page narrative:

> The difference in perspective which a change of beds made was enormous . . . In the bed next to the window it did indeed come about that I was relieved of these petty annoyances (N.B.: Annoyances caused by Laird and her roommate's perception that more space was needed between them), but this relief was scarcely noticed in my joy at attaining a new view of the outdoors . . . When the "morning girl" opened the drapes shortly before sunrise I could watch the growing light turn its delicate tracery of bare brown branches to rosy gold; and the same transformation took place towards sunset, except that then the color was deeper, verging on copper. To gaze at this tree in its semitropical setting at all hours and in all lights, never twice quite the same, afforded me the most exquisite pleasure that I experienced in all that drab period . . . From the vantage point of the bed by the window I felt much closer to the world of ongoing life, the world which held other things besides age and mental aberration and pre-occupation with dreary physical routines. (Laird, 1979, pp. 142-144)

Here is a first-hand account of the importance of a particular environmental factor—the situation of a resident's bed—and its direct effect on her outlook on life. This passage also introduces, from the resident's point of view, the unhomelike atmosphere of the home. Nursing homes look nothing like what anyone would call "home," or what residents remember as "home." Long corridors, dayrooms in which residents eat food from plastic dishes set on plastic trays, nursing stations and double-bedded rooms for non-related adults to share are attributes that no one in American culture would associate with their family home. What is generally found in most nursing homes are decorations and color schemes which attempt to convey a "homey" atmosphere. Laird writes about the visitor's introduction to Golden Mesa, the nursing home where she lived. "The anxious seekers who came to Golden Mesa were duly reassured by the charming entry way. Husband and wife might murmur to one another, 'You see, dear, it isn't in the least like those dreadful places we read about.' 'No, indeed, everything looks very homelike.' Then the Grasshopper Lady (N.B.: the administrator) in person would give them a tour of the institution, pointing out desirable features: the bright rooms, the well-made beds with attractive colored spreads, the cheerful dining room which was also a social hall, and the various recreational facilities. Along with the tour guide patter came the hypnotically repeated assurance, I'm sure he (or she, or they) will adjust nicely and be very happy here." (Laird, 1979 p. 124)

Stafford (1995) critiques the concrete embodiment of the idea of home in nursing homes in terms of the concept of memory. He argues that gerontology, in general, uses an overly representational model of memory rather than a model of memory as cultural legacy which includes imagination, emotion and insight. An individual's memory is about relationships, the experience of work, the feel of implements in one's hands, the sound of voices of loved ones and the myriad other daily experiences of life. Much of this kind of memory is erased after one enters the nursing home.

> So it's not only the erasure of memory, but the difficulty of making new memories which drains the nursing home of meaning. Granted, nursing home professionals try hard to create environments which might be considered homelike. Yet, the effort often fails due to the insufficient understanding of the foundation of memory cited earlier in the paper. As they understand memory to be cognitive-representational and symbolic, an attempt is made to create home by means of simulacrum. Hence, home is taken to be represented by wingback chairs, false fireplace hearths, country curtains and reminiscences about some generic mother's chocolate chip cookies. Farm implements and old time kitchen gadgets hung on the wall might be fun to talk about, but they don't make for home. As such, it trivialized the notion of home and, indeed, often has the opposite effect on the resident. The attempt to recreate home draws attention to its impossibility. (Stafford, 1995, pp. 9-10)

The gardening program at Riverview helps residents create new memories. This is especially evident when residents garden in the nursing home courtyard in summer. A recent addition to the courtyard gardening area is a mixed annual and perennial flower bed along a white fence which separates the courtyard from the neighborhood street. Program volunteers planned and planted this bed three years ago over my objections. I had wanted all of the resident gardening areas to be wheelchair accessible. We already had a number of wheelchair accessible planters and several large plastic pots in which all of the participants could plant. The volunteers insisted a flower garden in the ground next to the fence was exactly what the courtyard needed. And they were right.

Everyone who enters the courtyard loves the flower border. It contains almost 50 feet of perennials passed along to us, like the perennials in the backyards in the small town where Riverside is located. Along with the perennials–daylilies, hollyhocks, lythrum and coreopsis–there are colorful annuals–zinnias, asters, alyssum and cosmos. During the summer of the border's creation, I realized residents loved it so much because it was like the gardens everywhere else in town. This part of nursing home life reflected a normal part of town life. The flower border helped to normalize one part of the residents' lives in the nursing home. Each resident gardener saw the grassy area by the fence transformed into a profusion of bloom, partly from annuals they had raised from seed. The residents were aware of how much staff and visitors admired the flower border, as well as the vegetables and herbs in the planters. The residents helped to create these beautiful and delicious products, as well as new memories which helped to give meaning to their daily lives in the nursing home.

POVERTY AND NURSING HOME LIFE

Most individuals in America can count on having fewer economic resources the longer they live beyond retirement age. National statistics on age, sex and income indicate a significant drop in income with retirement. Older males have larger retirement incomes than females, but incomes continue to drop as individuals age. Females living alone have the lowest incomes (U.S. Bureau of the Census, 1991). In addition, the largest percentage (54%) of older people living alone are women 85 years of age and older (U.S. Bureau of the Census, 1990). With these statistics in mind, it is important to remember that the risk of a long nursing home stay is mainly dependent on social support, not degree of illness or disability. "Extrapolating from available data, we estimate that for every person over the age 65 in a nursing home there are from one to three people equally disabled living in the community. The importance of social support must be kept continuously in mind" (Kane et al., 1989, p. 36). It is no surprise that older women who are single or widowed, childless and poor are at the greatest risk of institutionalization. If one is not poor when one enters a nursing home, most long-stay residents can count on being pauperized while in the institution. The typical charge for care in a double occupancy nursing home room at Riverview and other homes in the area is about $50,000 per year. Because of these high costs, the great majority of Riverview residents qualify for Medicaid payment of nursing home care upon entering the home or fairly soon afterwards.

Kayser-Jones' (1981) comparative analysis of nursing home life in a California home and one in Scotland is particularly interesting in terms of the impact of poverty and lack of material resources on residents' lives. Through exchange theory analysis, Kayser-Jones concludes that the residents in the American home are more dependent and powerless than those in the Scottish home because they are so impoverished. The Americans not only have comparatively less money allocated to them by the state, but they also have fewer opportunities to make things which are valued by others or to buy small gifts in a shop on the premises than do the women in the Scottish home. For example, although the women in the home in Scotland have no activity director, they make things such as trays, padded coat hangers, childrens' toys and knitted scarves which they can sell or give to others. In the American home, an activity director plans many activities such as bingo, table games, musical entertainment, films, church services and parties. People win small prizes at bingo, but they are considered of little value by the residents and the activity director.

In the gardening program at Riverview, a major winter activity has been the propagation of house plant cuttings. In spring, annual flowers and tomato plants are propagated. We have two three-tiered light stands which create an abundance of propagated plants under the fluorescent lights. At the end of most winter sessions, residents are asked if they would like to take one or two plants with them. If they take the plants, the resident gardeners often give these as gifts to family, friends and staff. A resident said one evening as she eyed a particularly handsome philodendron under the lights, "I would love to give that plant to my granddaughter. She has been so sick, and I know it would make her feel better." Helen left with the plant on her lap, happy because she knew this plant would be seen as a significant gift. On another occasion, I wheeled Ken back to his room with a flowering potted geranium in his hands. Before we got to his room, he gave it to one of the nurses on his floor. She was delighted. I discovered that it was her turn to receive one of the plants that he always brought back from our weekly sessions. He explained to me that he never kept the plants from the gardening program for himself, but gave them to the nurses who worked so hard and liked them so much.

The biggest plant giveaway of the gardening program occurred when the surplus tomato seedlings were ready to find new homes. Those resident gardeners who knew someone who wanted seedlings were welcome to take as many as they could carry to their room. It became clear to me that the gardening program gave these residents something of value to give to others, something which increased their control over a valuable resource, and something which helped them feel some power, albeit modest, in the exchange of goods and services—activities central to American life.

I would like to interject a caution about the notion of work by nursing home residents. Many of the women and men who participated in our gardening program had been factory employees during much of their adult lives. Most factories in the town paid employees by piece work, so fast and careful work was a source of pride for many of these retired workers. A few of the residents likened the gardening program to work. Amy, for example, who had the use of only one hand, would often say, "I need more work," when she wanted us to give her more ivy cuttings for the pots she had ready for cuttings, or when she needed more of the materials for the project we were working on that day. She was a prodigious and cheerful worker. She loved the gardening program for the productive work it provided and because she loved to take plants back to her room to enjoy and to show her visitors what she had accomplished. In this sense, the gardening program provided meaningful and useful work for some of the residents.

On the other hand, residents seem very ambivalent about work done for the institution. The following is an illustrative example. The gardening group usually made holiday decorations in December. The activity director and I purchased small baubles, bangles, tinsel and lengths of artificial greenery for the session. Each resident made a spray or wreath according to her own fancy which she then took with her after the session. Most residents used these colorful and imaginative articles to decorate their bedrooms. One December, after we discussed the objectives of the session, the new activity director offered to purchase these materials on her own. At the beginning of the holiday decoration session, the director produced three very large artificial wreaths and fruit decorations. When I asked why she had made this unusual choice of materials, she said she thought it would be nice if the residents decorated wreaths for the outside doors of the home. We proceeded with the session. After we completed the project, the volunteers said many congratulatory words to the residents about the beautifully decorated wreaths. None of the residents seemed very pleased. The residents knew that they had been used or, at the very least, that our traditional holiday session had not had the individual and creative outcome enjoyed in the past. I learned an important lesson. One must be careful not to put institutional goals before residents' goals in activities in which the residents' needs are supposed to take precedence. Residents know when this occurs and will respond accordingly.

DISCUSSION

In light of the conceptual framework outlined above, let us return to the introductory paragraphs describing the photo of the two women and their colorful tulips. The following are some of my insights about the women in the photo:

1. We see the women as individual persons and as successful participants in gardening, a ubiquitous American pastime which is also part of their lives in the nursing home.
2. A common bond of friendship is acknowledged in their achievement. These women continued to build relationships while in the nursing home. As the program coordinator, I am aware the gardening program helped to strengthen the friendship between them through a shared, common interest.
3. The successful tulip project is so important to these two women that they had a family member record it. The photo reifies the achievement and preserves the moment for future reference. These women continue to be included in social relationships and networks beyond the nursing home in which they reside.
4. The gift of a photo is given to me, the gardening coordinator, in exchange for my contribution to the tulip planting project. It is a concrete reminder of these women's continued participation in reciprocal exchange relationships.
5. The women are making memories; they are creating meaning for themselves within the life of the nursing home. The commemorative photo taken of themselves together with the flowers they grew is an indication of the importance of this achievement and of their friendship which is framed by the tulips.

CONCLUSION

A sociocultural understanding of the basis for care in nursing homes and in health care of older people in general is increasingly perceived as unimportant and secondary by practitioners. Reimbursement systems which emphasize medicine and positive medical outcomes as the only ones that count have become preeminent in health policy. This predominantly biomedical perspective influences the way in which all types of practitioners define quality care. This paper attempts to demonstrate to horticultural therapists and others working in residential programs for older adults that, with respect to the feelings and experiences of the older people themselves, there is good evidence that sociocultural approaches to therapeutic work in nursing homes are more effective and compassionate.

An interpretation of therapeutic work based on these broader social understandings is necessary to therapeutic work with residents/clients and in interpersonal relations among staff because:

1. There is a tendency for nursing home professionals and others who work in health care to emphasize psychological interpretations of individual behavior. The focus for explanation of all types of phenomena is often on the individual rather than on systemic, environmental or historic factors. When there is difficulty with a program or a participant, practitioners often see causes rooted in personality differences, lack of individual initiative or the myriad other psychological interpretations projected onto individuals or groups of individuals, rather than on social causes, particularly the institutional framework for care.
2. Awareness by the therapist of the broader social and economic influences on institutional care allows the therapist to see her/himself within a complex set of conditions and constraints in health care. This broader understanding can be the foundation for a more active stance within the institutional setting, in addition to setting a framework for client advocacy.
3. These broader understandings can be the basis for better therapeutic interactions with clients and better therapy outcomes since a sociocultural framework provides the therapist with a more holistic approach to clients. A better understanding of the context of the lives of clients facilitates a better understanding of, for instance, the reasons certain interventions are ineffective or why a client's willingness to participate can seem so unpredictable.

REFERENCES

Baldwin, N., Harris, J., and Kelly, D. (1993). Institutionalisation: Why blame the institution? *Aging and Society,* 13, pp. 69-81.

Calkins, M.P. (1988). *Design for dementia: Planning environments for the elderly and the confused.* Owings Mills, MD: National Health Publishing.

Cohen, U. and Day, K. (1993). *Contemporary environments for people with dementia.* Baltimore: Johns Hopkins University Press.

Estes, C.L. and Binney, E.A. (1989). The biomedicalization of aging: Dangers and dilemmas. *Gerontologist, 29(5),* pp. 587-596.

Goffman, E. (1961). *Asylums.* Garden City: Anchor Books.

Gubrium, J.F. (1975). *Living and dying at Murray Manor.* New York: St. Martin's Press.

Hoglund, J.D. (1985). *Housing for the elderly: Privacy and independence in environments for the aging.* New York: Van Nostrand Reinhold.

Kane, R.L., Ouslander, J. G., and Abrass, I.B. (1989). *Essentials of clinical geriatrics.* Second edition. New York: McGraw-Hill.

Kayser-Jones, J. (1981). *Old, alone, and neglected. Care of the aged in Scotland and the United States.* Berkeley: University of California Press.

Koncelik, J.A. (1976). *Designing the open nursing home.* Stroudsburg, PA: Dowden, Hutchinson & Ross, Inc.

Laird, C. (1979). *Limbo.* Novato, CA: Chandler & Sharp Publishers.

Regnier, V. (1994). *Assisted living housing for the elderly: Design innovations from the United States and Europe.* New York: Van Nostrand Reinhold.

Rubinstein, R.L., Kilbride, J.C., and Nagy, S. (1992). *Elders living alone: Frailty and the perception of choice.* New York: Aldine De Gruyter.

Rybczynski, W. (1986). *Home: A short history of an idea.* New York: Viking Penguin.

Savishinsky, J.S. (1991). *The ends of time: Life and work in a nursing home.* New York: Bergin & Garvey.

Stafford, P.B. (1995). Memory in the here and now. Paper presented at the American Anthropological Association Annual Meeting. Washington, DC.

Thomas, W.H. (1994). *The Eden alternative: Nature, hope and nursing homes.* Columbia: University of Missouri.

U.S. Bureau of the Census. (1990). *Current Population Reports, Series P-20.* Washington, DC: U.S. Government Printing Office.

U.S. Bureau of the Census. (1991). *Current Population Reports, Series P-60.* Washington, DC: U.S. Government Printing Office.

Vladeck, B. (1980). *Unloving care: The nursing home tragedy.* New York: Basic Books.

Horticultural Therapy Education and Older Adults

Sharon Simson
Rebecca Haller

SUMMARY. Horticulture has been identified as the number one leisure pursuit of older Americans and as a therapeutic activity which enhances physical and mental health. Instrumental to the involvement of older adults with horticulture is the professional horticultural therapist (HT). Horticultural therapist education, competency skills and professional challenges related to older persons are explored using data from two surveys. The primary method used is a 42-item survey administered in 1995 to 33 American Horticultural Therapy Association (AHTA) members who reported specialties in "education" and "older adults" in the AHTA 1994 Directory. A secondary method is a 55-item question survey administered in 1994 to directors of 41 educational programs associated with AHTA (return rate 76%). Specific topics discussed include educational programs that address aging in their curricula; competencies that should be taught with specific content on older adults; the importance of

---

Sharon Simson, PhD, is Instructor of Plant Science at Harcum College, Bryn Mawr, PA, and Adjunct Professor of Gerontology at University of Maryland University College. Address correspondence to: Forevergreen, 768 Mustin Lane, Villanova, PA 19085.

Rebecca Haller, HTM, is Manager, Horticultural Therapy Program, Denver Botanic Gardens. Address correspondence to: Denver Botanic Gardens, 909 York Street, Denver, CO 80206.

An earlier version of this paper was presented at the 1995 Annual Conference of the American Horticultural Therapy Association in Montreal.

[Haworth co-indexing entry note]: "Horticultural Therapy Education and Older Adults." Simson, Sharon, and Rebecca Haller. Co-published simultaneously in *Activities, Adaptation & Aging* (The Haworth Press, Inc.) Vol. 22, No. 3, 1997, pp. 125-140; and: *Horticultural Therapy and the Older Adult Population* (ed: Suzanne E. Wells) The Haworth Press, Inc., 1997, pp. 125-140. Single or multiple copies of this article are available for a fee from The Haworth Document Delivery Service [1-800-342-9678, 9:00 a.m. - 5:00 p.m. (EST). E-mail address: getinfo@haworth.com].

125

introductory gerontology courses in HT curriculum; and future challenges in teaching about older adults in terms of curriculum, faculty, students, and employment. Survey results provide a basis for proposing ways in which the HT profession can enhance its educational programs to address the future needs of a growing population of older adults. *[Article copies available for a fee from The Haworth Document Delivery Service: 1-800-342-9678. E-mail address: getinfo@haworth.com]*

Horticulture is identified as a leisure pursuit of over 68 million households in the United States and as a therapeutic activity that enhances physical and mental health (Gallup Organization, 1994; Relf, 1992). Millions of older adults enjoy tending their own flower or vegetable gardens or indoor plant collections. Many others participate in group activities such as garden clubs, community garden associations, plant societies, arboretum and botanic garden programs, and county extension programs. For an increasing number of older adults, gardening is an essential therapeutic activity which aids in health maintenance and rehabilitation from acute or chronic illnesses including stroke, broken bones caused by falls, depression, cancer, substance abuse and respiratory ailments (Relf, 1992; Rothert & Daubert, 1980-1981).

Instrumental to the involvement of older adults with therapeutic horticulture is the professional horticultural therapist (HT). Horticultural therapists utilize plants and horticultural activities to improve the social, educational, psychological, and physical adjustment of persons while improving their body, mind and spirits (Stevenson et al., 1995). HTs face a challenge in adapting and applying horticultural therapy concepts and skills to the needs of the older population.

Elderly people are the fastest growing segment of the U.S. population; every eighth American is age 65 or older and there will be 35.3 million older adults by the year 2000. Most older persons have at least one chronic illness and find their usual activities restricted 34 days per year because of illness or injury. Elderly people account for 35% of hospital stays and 47% of all days of care in hospitals (AARP, 1995). Over 60% of the American public has some experience with long-term care that includes a range of health, personal care and social services for individuals lacking certain functional capacities (AARP, 1988).

Over the years, the relationship between HT and older adults has been explored and a growing body of literature has been produced. A pioneering series of monographs issued by the Chicago Horticultural Society explored HT in various practice settings including nursing homes, senior centers, psychiatric hospitals, retirement homes and rehabilitation facilities (Rothert & Daubert, 1980-1981). Instructions on how to develop therapeutic horticultural programs for older adults in these and other settings have been presented in guidebooks for practicing professionals and volunteer leaders (Peckham and Peckham, 1982; Saxon and Etten, 1984; Moore, 1989).

Horticulture has been employed widely to treat and to promote both physical and mental health (Riordin and Williams, 1988). The use of horticultural or gardening activities with institutionalized older adults has been examined in terms of rationales for use, benefits to patients, promotion of overall wellness, and recreation and socialization purposes (Breed, 1986; Burgess, 1990; Catlin, 1992). Older persons with Alzheimer's disease have benefited from participation in horticultural activities and therapeutically designed garden areas (Kromm and Kromm Young, 1985; Namazi and Haynes, 1994). Older adults have been able to expand their options in later life through horticulture related opportunities such as continuing education, recreational pursuits and new careers (Van Zandt and Peterson, 1980; Dellman Jenkins and Papalia, 1985; Brewer, 1987; and Beisgen, 1989).

To work effectively with older adults, HTs require an appropriate educational background acquired in both classroom and practice settings (Simson and Straus, 1995). The current HT core curriculum used by the American Horticultural Therapy Association (AHTA) Registration Review Board includes over 40 courses divided into four categories: HT specialization, horticultural science, therapy/human science and management (Table 1). As a professional organization refining its core educational curriculum for its proposed certification program, AHTA is in a position to determine the specialized knowledge and skills essential to HTs who practice with the older adult population.

Research which focuses specifically on the education of horticultural therapists related to older adults remains undeveloped. This study seeks to contribute to knowledge in this area by exploring four questions about HT education related to older adults:

1. Are aging populations a focus of courses in HT educational programs?
2. How important is an introductory gerontology course in HT education?
3. What HT competencies (knowledge and skills) should be taught with specific content on older adults?
4. What are the future challenges for HT in teaching about older adults in terms of curriculum, faculty, students and employment?

This study is significant because it contributes to the ongoing effort of the horticultural therapy profession to design an educational curriculum and a

TABLE 1. Horticultural Therapy Core Curriculum of the American Horticultural Therapy Association, January 1, 1991

        The Core Curriculum is used by the AHTA Registration Review Board to assign point values to the various educational experiences of applicants for professional registration, and may guide the student in a course of study in Horticultural Therapy. For registration; degreed, non-degreed and continuing education course work is evaluated as outlined in the procedures with reference to this document. Following are the topics from which to select, and the total semester credits required in each category.

- **HORTICULTURAL THERAPY SPECIALIZATION COURSES**

  - Introduction to Horticultural Therapy
  - Horticultural Therapy Techniques (includes adaptive gardens/tools, etc.)
  - Horticultural Therapy Programming (i.e., assessment, goal planning, task analysis, horticulture activity, planning documentation, etc.)
  - Special Topics in Horticultural Therapy (includes: funding, working with volunteers, research, grant writing, etc.)
  - Internship–1000 hours (6 months) required credits may vary

  Semester Credits Required   **8 + Internship**

- **HORTICULTURAL SCIENCE AND RELATED COURSES**

  - Introduction to Horticulture
  - Plant Propagation
  - Plant Materials
  - Greenhouse or Nursery Production/Management
  - Landscape Design/Construction
  - Introductory Botany
  - Basic Soil Science
  - Entomology
  - Plant Pathology
  - Plant Physiology
  - Fruit and Vegetable Crops/Gardening
  - Basic Floral Design/Horticultural Crafts
  - Specialization Plants (herbs, turfgrass, interior, rock gardening, ferns, etc.)

  Semester Credits Required   **40**

- **THERAPY/HUMAN SCIENCE COURSES**

  - Introductory Psychology
  - Abnormal Psychology
  - Introductory Sociology
  - Courses specializing in one of these areas: physical disabilities, developmental disabilities, emotional disabilities, geriatrics, corrections, psychiatric, community based programs, etc.
  - Courses in the following subjects: Multiple Disabilities, Group Dynamics/Process, Counseling, Vocational, Rehabilitation, Special Education, Recreation/Therapeutic Skills and Services, Educational Psychology, Anatomy/Physiology, Sign Language, First Aid/CPR, Crisis Intervention

  Semester Credits Required   24

- **MANAGEMENT COURSES**

  - Communication/Public Speaking
  - Research Methods/Statistics
  - Computers
  - Business Management/Economics

  Semester Credits Required   6

  Minimum Total Semester Credits Required   78 + Internship

certification program that will enhance HT capabilities to address present and future needs of a growing older adult population.

METHOD

The primary method used in this research was a 42-item survey, "HT Education and Older Adults," administered in 1995 to 33 AHTA members who reported specialization in both "education" and "older adults" in the AHTA 1994 Directory. The total number of respondents was 25, or a 76%

rate of return. The mail questionnaire contained both forced choice and open-ended questions exploring these areas: (a) The importance of an introductory gerontology course in HT education; (b) HT competencies (knowledge and skills) that should be taught with specific content on older adults; and (c) future challenges for HT in teaching about older adults in terms of curriculum, faculty, students and employment. The questions on HT competencies were based on a list generated by focus groups at the 1991 AHTA National Conference. The questions on future challenges were formulated by specialists in gerontology and horticultural therapy who are knowledgeable about practice, education and policy issues.

This primary method was supplemented by findings from a secondary method, a 55-item survey, "HT General Education." This questionnaire was administered in 1994 to directors of 41 educational programs associated with AHTA and had a 76% return rate (Simson & Straus, 1995). Respondents included institutions and facilities offering internship programs, universities and colleges offering horticultural therapy programs or courses, and botanical gardens/arboreta offering training related to horticultural therapy. This survey provides data about aging topics currently taught in curricula of educational programs and HT competencies that should be taught in all educational programs. The competency questions were identical to those used in the "HT Education and Older Adults" questionnaire.

RESULTS

Are aging populations a focus of courses in HT educational programs? The HT general education survey asked directors of HT education programs to identify the client populations addressed in their courses. Respondents reported that over 80% of HT educational programs address the geriatric population. This percentage places the geriatric population among the most frequently addressed populations along with the physically challenged, the mentally challenged and psychiatric. Geriatric populations are a focus of 12.1% of the 207 courses offered by respondents, second only to the most frequently cited focus of courses, the physically challenged (14%).

How important is an introductory gerontology course in HT education? Respondents to "HT Education and Older Adults" were asked to rate the importance of an introductory gerontology course in preparing HTs to work with older adults. The majority (68%) consider an introductory gerontology course "very important" (44%) or "important" (24%). Only a small percentage consider a course "unimportant" (8%) or "very unimportant" (4%).

Which HT competencies should be taught with specific content on older adults? Respondents to "HT Education and Older Adults" were asked: "Which HT competencies should be taught with specific content on older adults?" A list of 25 competencies was presented and respondents were asked to select the top ten competencies that should include specific content on older adults. Respondents identified accessible garden design as the most essential competency (84%) that should be taught with specific content on older adults. Following closely were adaptable tools and techniques (76%) and communication skills (76%). Six additional competencies were identified by at least 60% of respondents: basic first aid, basic horticulture crafts and patient assessment and documentation (64% each); and counseling skills and techniques, cognitive disabilities, and medications and their effects (60% each). In contrast, four competencies were selected by only 12% of respondents: human physiology, plant physiology, federal regulations, public relations and marketing.

The same set of competency questions was administered in the HT general education survey which asked, "What HT competencies should be taught in HT education?" Respondents identified counseling skills and techniques as the most essential competency to teach in HT education (83%), followed closely by patient assessment and documentation (80%). Six additional competencies were identified by at least 50% of respondents: adaptable tools and techniques, human psychology, accessible garden design, communication skills, greenhouse design and operations, and planting design and seasonal maintenance. In contrast, eight competencies were selected by less than 27% of respondents: entomology and pest control, basic floral design, basic first aid, federal regulations, public relations and marketing, poisonous plants, medications and their effects, and stroke and spinal cord injury.

Similarities and differences appear when findings from the two surveys are compared. Both surveys ranked these four competencies among their top six: patient assessment and documentation, adaptable tools and techniques, accessible garden design, and communication skills. Both surveys ranked federal regulations and public relations and marketing among the six least important competencies.

The frequency with which competencies were selected vary between the two surveys. Accessible garden design, the top choice in "HT Education and Older Adults" was selected by 84% of respondents, but by only 63% of respondents in the HT general education survey. The top choice in the general education survey, counseling skills and techniques, was se-

TABLE 2. Horticultural Therapy Competencies Selected by Respondents to HT General Education Survey and Respondents to HT Education and Older Adults Survey

Competencies	% older adult respondents who selected competency to be taught with specific content on older adults	% HT general education survey respondents who selected competency to be taught in HT general education
Accessible garden design	84	63
Adaptable tools and techniques	76	70
Communication skills	76	63
Basic first aid	64	23
Basic horticulture crafts	64	43
Patient assessment & documentation	64	80
Cognitive disabilities	60	37
Counseling skills and techniques	60	83
Medications and their effects	60	10
Planting design & seasonal maintenance	48	50
Human psychology	40	70
Herbaceous plant materials	36	47
Human growth and development	36	40
Basic floral design	32	27
Entomology and pest control	28	27
Greenhouse design and operations	28	50
Poisonous plants	28	13
Stroke and spinal cord injury	28	10
Basic medical terminology & knowledge	16	30
Budget preparation and management	16	33
Federal regulations	12	23
Human physiology	12	37
Plant physiology	12	30
Public relations and marketing	12	20
Other	12	17

Respondents = 25

lected by 83% of respondents but by only 60% in the older adults survey. In comparing the two surveys, a difference of at least 20% in response frequencies can be noted for 9 out of 25 competencies (Table 2).

What are the future challenges in teaching HTs about older adults? "HT Education and Older Adults" presented a check list of 15 challenges that explored teaching about older adults in terms of curriculum, faculty, students and employment. Respondents were asked: "The following list presents future challenges in educating HTs to work with older adults. Although all challenges may be important to you, please check the five challenges that you think are most important. Of the five challenges that you selected, which challenge is most important?"

The educational challenge selected most often was "design HT curriculum to incorporate specific content on older adults" (92% of respondents) (Table 3). Several other top choices, selected by approximately half of the respondents, included: "encourage HT students to take courses taught by other disciplines which incorporate specific content on older adults" (56%); "recruit faculty who have a specialty in aging to teach in HT education programs" (48%); "connect HT students with job opportunities with older adults" (48%); and "arrange HT internships in programs having older adult clients" (44%). Challenges selected by one third of respondents were: "increase number of HT educational programs that incorporate specific content on older adults" (36%); "offer HT continuing education on older adults" (32%); and "motivate employer to assist HTs who work with older adults to pursue continuing education related to older adults" (32%). Two challenges were selected by less than 10% of respondents: "standardize HT curriculum content on older adults," and "obtain external funding to develop content on older adults that could be incorporated into HT education."

When asked to select the single most important future challenge, respondents chose "designing HT curriculum to incorporate specific content on older adults" (32%) or "connecting HT students with job opportunities with older adults" (24%).

DISCUSSION AND RECOMMENDATIONS

The educational challenge selected by the largest percentage of respondents (92%) was "design HT curriculum to incorporate specific content on older adults." In order to address this challenge and to provide students with the specialty education needed to work with older adults, HT education programs could consider supplementing the general HT curriculum

TABLE 3. Future Educational Challenges Identified by Respondents to HT Education and Older Adults Survey

Educational challenges	% scoring challenge as important to HT education and older adults	Overall rank of challenge
Curriculum		
Design HT curriculum to incorporate specific content on older adults.	92	1
Standardize HT curriculum content on older adults.	8	14
Offer HT continuing education on older adults.	32	7
increase number of HT educational programs that incorporate specific content on older adults.	36	6
Obtain external funding to develop content on older adults that could be incorporated into HT education.	8	14
Faculty		
Secure faculty support for incorporating content on older persons in HT curriculum.	28	9
Recruit faculty who have a specialty in aging to teach in HT education programs.	48	3
Students		
Recruit students to take HT courses that incorporate specific content on older adults.	24	10
Encourage HT students to take courses taught by other disciplines which incorporate specific content on older adults.	56	2
Offer scholarships to students to pursue education and careers in HT with older adults.	12	12
Prepare students for test questions on older adults in the proposed HT certification exam.	20	11
Arrange HT internships in programs having older adult clients.	44	5

Educational challenges	% scoring challenge as important to HT education and older adults	Overall rank of challenge
Employment		
Connect HT students with job opportunities with older adults.	48	3
Motivate employers to assist HTs who work with older adults to pursue continuing education related to older adults.	32	7
Other challenges	12	13

Respondents = 25

with additional courses on older adults and incorporating content on older adults into existing HT courses.

Supplement the general HT curriculum with additional courses on older adults. Students planning careers with older adults could be required or encouraged to pursue gerontological courses. Core courses could include Introduction to Social Gerontology, Health and Aging, and the Psychology of Aging. Additional electives could be selected from such courses as Long Term Care, Public Policy, Economics of Aging and Senior Housing. These courses would probably need to be pursued through interdisciplinary and interdepartmental channels. At colleges which do not offer gerontological courses, it would be necessary for students to cross enroll at institutions where gerontological instruction is offered.

Incorporate content on older adults into existing HT courses. Content on older adults could be incorporated into existing horticultural therapy courses. This content could be formulated according to the principles set forth in a report by the Association of Gerontologists in Higher Education (AGHE) (Wendt, Peterson, & Douglas, 1993). This report identifies the core knowledge essential to professionals working with older persons.

Structure/Contexts/Heterogeneity

- Understand the variety of contexts within which aging can be examined and its implications for practice.
- Identify how older persons are affected by the human-environment interaction.

Concepts and Theories Used to Study Aging

- Identify and define/describe bio/psycho/social concepts and theories used to study aging.
- Recognize the influence of each theory on policies and procedures in practice.

Stability and Directions of Change

- Understand the trajectories of improvement or decrement in individual functioning.
- Identify various dynamics of the immediate interpersonal environment within which aging occurs.
- Recognize the reciprocal effects of aging on groups, social institutions and social policy over time.

Ethical Issues

- Appreciate that many ethical issues are important in the field of aging.
- Know and accept the ethics of professional practice in the field of aging.
- Appreciate the need for ethical accountability in practice.

Scholarship and Research

- Understand the importance of evaluating popular media representations of aging.
- Summarize professional and scientific literature in gerontology to maintain currency in knowledge and skills, to provide valid rationale for practice and policies, and to enhance accurate interpretation of the various aging processes for the public and other professionals.
- Understand how applied research can be utilized to improve practice.

Application/Practice

- Identify a range of services for elders available in most communities.
- Understand generally the division of labor among different agencies providing funding and services for elders.
- Understand the requisite practice skills appropriate to the intended area of gerontological practice.
- Understand the importance of program review and evaluation for program effectiveness.

TABLE 4. Horticultural Therapy Curriculum that Incorporates Content Related to Older Adults

HT COMPETENCY	HT LEARNING OBJECTIVES	HT CONTENT	OLDER ADULT LEARNING OBJECTIVES AND CONTENT
Accessible garden design	Provide information regarding components and requirements in order to design a garden that can be accessed and used by an individual, group or groups with varying abilities.	Americans with Disabilities Act information Client centered approach Surfaces (paths and walkways) Growing beds (sizes, heights, placements, proximity to building) Comfort (materials, sun/shade, seating) Safety Construction techniques and materials	Understand the variety of contexts within which aging can be examined and its implications for practice. Understand the trajectories of improvement and/or decrement in individual functioning.
Adaptable tools and techniques	Identify challenges, compensation and modification of tools and tasks to accommodate those served.	Strengths and challenges of populations served Compensation types (strength, grasp, modality, endurances) Tool adaptation Tool availability and selection Task structuring to compensate for disabilities Safety	Identify and define/describe bio/psycho/social concepts and theories used to study aging. Recognize the influence of each theory on policies and procedures in practice.
Counseling skills and techniques	Utilize technique to improve psychological adjustment.	Group process Behavior management Reality orientation Influences of life experiences	Identify various dynamics of the immediate interpersonal environment within which aging occurs. Identify a range of services for elders available in most communities.
Medications and their effects	Account for the effects of commonly prescribed medications.	Medications and their effects especially as related to sensitivities, sun tolerance, attention and endurance for garden safety	Recognize the influence of bio/psycho/social concepts and theories on policies and procedures in practice.

A horticultural therapy curriculum could be designed to incorporate any or all of the core knowledge suggested by the AGHE report. A model HT curriculum that encompasses HT competencies, HT learning objectives, HT content and older adult learning objectives and content is presented in Table 4. This curriculum could be implemented through several approaches: A cooperative arrangement between existing HT faculty with faculty who have expertise in aging; HT faculty who develop their own expertise in aging through continuing education; and visiting instructors who are experts in aging. Intended as an outline of topics to include in order to prepare students to work with this special population, the curriculum could also serve as a guideline for the design of continuing education programs, i.e., workshops and symposiums.

More rigorous educational requirements for practitioners working with older adults could enhance their potential for commanding higher financial compensation. According to recent salary surveys of AHTA members, horticultural therapists working in geriatrics have the lowest average salaries when compared with other horticultural therapists working with special populations (Professor Richard Mattson, Kansas State University, personal interview, 1995). Specialized educational preparation and formal credentials are required for many HTs who provide older adults medical or therapeutic services in health, long term care and day treatment facilities. To be considered part of a professional staff and to compete for higher salaries, HTs need an appropriate and rigorous educational background and credentials. Although salaries are influenced by a number of factors, educational credentials provide one rationale for designating the HT services provided to older adults as therapeutic and an integral component of health care that should be reimbursed.

REFERENCES

American Association of Retired Persons & Pacific Presbyterian Medical Center. (1988). *Aging in America: Issue Guide.* Washington, DC: AARP.

American Association of Retired Persons. (1995). *A Profile of Older Americans.* Washington, DC: AARP.

Beisgen, V.A. (1989). *Life-Enhancing Activities for Mentally Impaired Elders: A Practical Guide.* New York: Springer Publishing Co.

Breed, J. (1986). Flowering of horticulture at Amsterdam House. *Journal of Gerontological Social Work,* 9(3), 95-97.

Brewer, S. (1987). Turning your green thumb into a new career. *Fifty Plus, 27(10),* 27-31.

Burgess, C.W. (1990). Horticulture and its application to the institutionalized elderly. *Activities, Adaptation & Aging,* 14(3), 51-61.

Catlin, P.A., Milliorn, A.B. & Milliorn, M.R. (1992). Horticulture therapy promotes 'wellness,' autonomy in residents. *Provider, 18(7),* 40.

Delman Jenkins, M.M. & Papalia Finley, D. (1985). Continuing education in later adulthood: Implications for program development for elderly guest students. *International Journal of Aging and Human Development,* 20(2), 93-102.

Gallup Organization. (1994). *National Gardening Survey,* conducted for the National Association for Gardening.

Kromm, D. & Kromm Young, H.N. (1985). Nursing unit designed for Alzheimer's disease patients at Newton Presbyterian Manor. *Nursing Homes, 34(3),* 30-31.

Moore, B. (1989). *Growing with gardening: A twelve-month guide for therapy, recreation, and education.* Chapel Hill, NC: University of North Carolina Press.

Namazi, K.H. & Haynes, S.R. (1994). Sensory stimuli reminiscence for patients with Alzheimer's disease: Relevance and implications. *Clinical Gerontologist, 4(4),* 26-46.

Peckham, W.W. & Peckham, A.R. (1982). *Activities keep me going: A guidebook for activity personnel who plan, direct and evaluate activities with older persons.* Nashville, TN: Parthenon Press.

Relf, D. (Ed.). (1992). *The role of horticulture in human well-being and social development.* Portland, OR: Timber Press.

Riordan, R. & Williams, C.S. (1988). Gardening therapeutics for the elderly. *Activities, Adaptation & Aging,* 12(1/2), 103-111.

Rothert, E. & Daubert, J. (Eds.). (1980-1981). *Horticultural therapy for nursing homes, senior centers and retirement living; Horticultural therapy at a physical rehabilitation facility; Horticultural therapy at a psychiatric hospital; Horticultural therapy for the mentally handicapped.* Glencoe, IL: Chicago Horticultural Society, Horticultural Therapy Department.

Saxon, S.V. & Etten, M.J. (1984). *Psychosocial rehabilitative programs for older adults.* Springfield, IL: Thomas.

Simson, S.P. & Straus, M.C. (1995). *Sowing the seeds, reaping the harvest: Horticultural therapy education for today and tomorrow.* Gaithersburg, MD: American Horticultural Therapy Association.

Stevenson, N., Davis, S., Straus, M., & Simson, S. (1995). *Case statement.* Gaithersburg, MD: American Horticultural Therapy Association.

VanZandt, S. & Peterson, D.A. (1980). Golden age 4-H clubs: An experience in adult education. *Lifelong Learning, 4(3),* 18-21.

Wendt, P.F., Peterson, D.A. & Douglas, E.B. (1993). *Core principles and outcomes of gerontology, geriatrics and aging studies instruction.* Washington, DC: Association of Gerontology in Higher Education.

Behavioral Study of Youth and Elders in an Intergenerational Horticultural Program

Jack Kerrigan
Nancy C. Stevenson

SUMMARY. Specified, discrete behaviors (verbal and nonverbal, academic and social) of youth and elders in an intergenerational horticultural program were observed and recorded for a 12-week period. The behaviors were modified from a set of behaviors designated for standardized observations in the "Generations Together" program developed and managed by Dr. Sally Newman of the University of Pittsburgh. The youth, ages nine to 11 years, come from public and parochial schools for an after school program. The elders are volunteers from a neighborhood center congregate program. Pairings were made at the beginning of the study period and were maintained through the study. The horticultural and horticultural

---

Jack Kerrigan, MA, is Assistant Professor and Extension Agent, Horticulture and Natural Resources, Ohio State University Extension, Cuyahoga County, 2490 Lee Boulevard, Suite 108, Cleveland Heights, OH 44118-1255. Internet address kerrigan.1@osu.edu

Nancy C. Stevenson, BA, HTR, is Consulting Horticultural Therapist, Green Encounters, 2268 Ardleigh Drive, Cleveland Heights, OH 44106.

The authors acknowledge and thank Dr. Sally Newman, Executive Director and Barbara Larimer of Generations Together, an intergenerational studies program, University Center for Social and Urban Research, University of Pittsburgh, for their guidance and assistance in this project and for the analysis of the data.

The Evans Family Foundation provided financial support for the project.

[Haworth co-indexing entry note]: "Behavioral Study of Youth and Elders in an Intergenerational Horticultural Program." Kerrrigan, Jack, and Nancy C. Stevenson. Co-published simultaneously in *Activities, Adaptation & Aging* (The Haworth Press, Inc.) Vol. 22, No. 3, 1997, pp. 141-153; and: *Horticultural Therapy and the Older Adult Population* (ed: Suzanne E. Wells) The Haworth Press, Inc., 1997, pp. 141-153. Single or multiple copies of this article are available for a fee from The Haworth Document Delivery Service [1-800-342-9678, 9:00 a.m. - 5:00 p.m. (EST). E-mail address: getinfo@haworth.com].

141

craft curriculum was designed by the registered horticultural therapists on staff at the Cleveland Botanical Garden with Nancy Stevenson, HTR. Observations were conducted by Jack Kerrigan, Extension Agent, Horticulture, Ohio State University Extension, Cuyahoga County and Nancy C. Stevenson, HTR. Behavioral observation data were compiled and analyzed by the "Generations Together" program. *[Article copies available for a fee from The Haworth Document Delivery Service: 1-800-342-9678. E-mail address: getinfo@ haworth.com]*

The Cleveland Botanical Garden (CBG), the Goodrich-Gannett Neighborhood Center (GGNC), Generations Together (GT) (an Intergenerational Studies Program in the University of Pittsburgh's Center for Social and Urban Research) and the Horticulture Program of Ohio State University Extension, Cuyahoga County, Ohio (OSUE) all united to study the effects of an intergenerational horticultural/gardening program on the participants.

The Goodrich-Gannett Neighborhood Center serves a neighborhood of more than 20,000 residents with a poverty rate (family of four earning less than $13,950 per year) of more than 63%. The primary goal of the three-year pilot intergenerational gardening project was to promote positive interaction between senior citizens and elementary school children in the neighborhoods served by GGNC through gardening and related craft projects.

Many older adults have limited income and resources resulting in a sense of loss of control over their lives and their world. Many experience a fear for personal safety at home and in the community leading to isolation and decreased independence. The children are often seen as responsible for crime in their neighborhood and thus deserving of punishment. Neighborhood children lack an understanding and appreciation of elders, especially those of different racial or ethnic backgrounds. There are very few opportunities for the two generations to come together in a positive and meaningful way. Both children and elders need nurturing, a sense of self-esteem and a sense of self-worth.

The Cleveland Botanical Garden and the Goodrich-Gannett Neighborhood Center designed a 3-year intergenerational horticulture project for youth ages 9 to 11 participating in GGNC's after-school program and senior citizens active in GGNC's senior programs. Generations Together provided a validated tool for observing behaviors during the study period by trained observers, Jack Kerrigan and Nancy C. Stevenson, HTR. The Horticulture Program of Ohio State University Extension in Cuyahoga

County, OH provided volunteer Master Gardeners to work with the horticultural therapists and staff from CBG.

The three-year project was a year-round program of outdoor gardening, indoor gardening with light carts and horticulturally-related crafts and activities. The project goal was to promote positive meaningful and nurturing interaction between elders and elementary age children through horticulture. Key components of this goal were: (a) to promote self-sufficiency and self-esteem in both the elders and children; (b) to encourage healthy, active socialization among the different age groups; (c) to increase participants' knowledge and appreciation of horticulture and the environment and to foster stewardship of the environment; (d) to provide mild physical exercise in a restorative setting; (e) to teach new skills (vocabulary, language and nutrition) that can be used at school and in the home; (f) to provide the elders an opportunity to teach and nurture children; (g) to help children understand and value elders in the community; and (h) to help the elders increase their acceptance of children while decreasing their fear of isolation.

The study period was the late winter indoor portion of the program's third year. Until the study, adults and youth self-selected partners each week. During the study, pairing of youth and elders were made by the staff of GGNC.

METHODS

Each session began with the activity being explained to the elders by the horticultural therapy facilitators. The elders then did the activity. The students were then brought into the room and seated with their elder. An introduction to the activity and basic instructions were given by the facilitators. The elders took over and guided their student partner through the activity. At the end of the activity, the facilitator asked questions and encouraged the students to write a summary of the activity in their journal.

The horticultural and horticultural craft curriculum was designed by Nancy C. Stevenson, HTR; Libby Reavis, HTR; and Shirley Badger, Ph.D. and a Master Gardener volunteer. Most sessions consisted of two activities. There were a total of 16 craft activities and 19 plant growing related activities (see Table 1).

An instrument developed by Sally Newman, Ph.D., of Generations Together was modified to fit the horticultural activities to be observed. The instrument consisted of a series of observable behaviors (see Table 2) divided into two major groups, verbal academic/social and nonverbal academic/social. The recorders (Nancy Stevenson and Jack Kerrigan) ob-

TABLE 1

Week	Horticultural Activities	Craft Activities
1	Plant Structure; start bean and squash seeds	Seed mosaics, name tags
2	Check growth of seeds, soil composition, fertilizer, worm composting bin	——
3	Plan flower garden, select seeds	Seed collages
4	——	Valentine corsages and cards
5	Plan vegetable garden, window sill herb garden	——
6	Sow seeds, take cuttings and plant desert dish garden	——
7	Repot plants, sow seeds	——
8	Divide and pot houseplants, beneficial insects	——
9	Sow seeds, observe seeds with microscope	Make flower lotto game
10	Transplant seedlings, sow seeds	——
11	Transplant seedlings	——
12	——	Flower arranging

served a specific intergenerational pair for six 30-second periods, recording all behaviors observed. The 30-second observation periods were conducted at the beginning, middle and end of each project. Observed behaviors were only recorded once during any single 30-second observation period even if they occurred repeatedly.

The data were collected over a 12-week period. A total of 35 elder/youth interaction segments were observed. Generations Together staff then analyzed the data from the observations to provide averages for each behavior.

RESULTS

Generally, behavioral interactions increased over the twelve-week period. This was particularly true for both elders and students regarding looking at each other, smiling, helping and speaking spontaneously and calmly. Student behaviors increasing dramatically over the 12 weeks included expression of satisfaction, interest and asking questions.

TABLE 2. Gardening Program Interaction Analysis Instrument

Names_____Activity_____

Date_____   Indoor/Outdoor

Category Verbal Academic / Social   Seconds

OBSERVABLE BEHAVIOR	30	30	30	30	30	30
EInst Elder provides instruction						
EQ Elder asks questions						
EAns Elder answers questions						
ECI Elder clarifies instruction						
SQ Student asks question						
SAns Student answers question						
SHelp Student asks for help						
ERev Elder engages in personal inquiry						
EHelp Elder offers help						
ECorr Elder corrects student's work						
EBeh Elder corrects student's behavior						
ECalm Elder talks calmly to student						
SInt Student expresses interest						
SSat Student expresses satisfaction						
SDis Student expresses dissatisfaction						
SCalm Student talks calmly to elder						
EInq Elder engages in personal inquiry						
EPr Elder praises student						
EEnc Elder encourages student						
ESpont Elder talks spontaneously						
SInq Student responds to personal inquiry						
SPr Student responds to praise						
SEnc Student responds to encouragement						
SSpont Student talks spontaneously						

TABLE 2 (continued)

Names_____Activity_____

Date_____   Indoor/Outdoor

Category Nonverbal Academic / Social   Seconds

OBSERVABLE BEHAVIOR–Elders	30	30	30	30	30	30
Eprep Elder prepares materials						
EHelp Elder helps student						
EDem Elder demonstrates by example						
SCr Student creates, but not engaged						
SAt Student attends to task, engaged in task						
SGest Student gesticulates						
SHelp Student helps elder						
ETouch Elder touches student						
ELk Elder looks at student						
ESm Elder smiles at student						
STouch Student touches elder						
SLk Student looks at elder						
SSm Student smiles at elder						

Several behaviors were observed only infrequently throughout the 12-week program: student helping elder; student expressing dissatisfaction; student responding to praise; student responding to personal inquiry; elder engaging in personal inquiry; student responding to encouragement; student touching elder; elder touching student. Elders were specifically instructed by the Neighborhood Center staff not to touch students because of the potential for liability. In addition, elders rarely corrected student behavior because Goodrich-Gannett staff were always present to address behavioral problems.

Figures 1 through 10 depict the mean observations for the behaviors over the 12-week study period.

The activities of planning the garden and sowing seeds (week 5) and potting geranium cuttings and planting desert dish gardens (week 6) generated the greatest interactions on the part of both the elders and the students. These activities provided the greatest opportunity for positive interaction, as evidenced by the greater frequency of behaviors exhibited by both elder and youth participants.

When comparing horticultural craft activities to gardening-related activities, the data suggest that more behaviors occurred during the gardening-related activities than during the craft-related activities. The patterns are similar across the 37 behaviors being observed. Both elders and students exhibited more interactions, especially in the categories "elder helps student," "elder talks calmly to student," "student expresses interest," "student talks calmly to elder," "elder demonstrates for student," "elder provides instruction," "elder talks spontaneously," "elder offers help and student looks at elder." Figure 11 shows the comparison of the mean frequency of the observations during craft and horticultural/gardening classifications of activities.

FIGURE 1. Mean Observations of Elder Verbal Academic/Social Behaviors

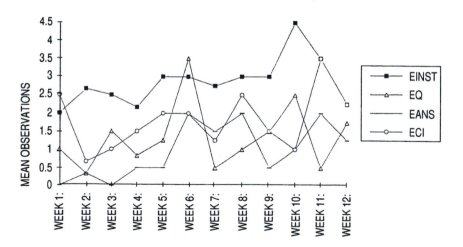

FIGURE 2. Mean Observations of Student Verbal Academic/Social Behaviors

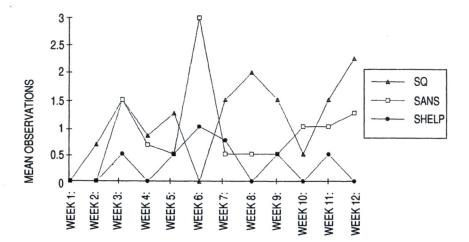

FIGURE 3. Mean Observations of Elder Verbal Academic/Social Behaviors

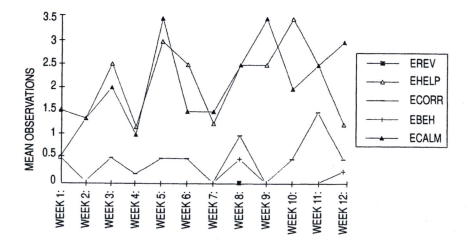

FIGURE 4. Mean Observations of Student Verbal Academic/Social Behaviors

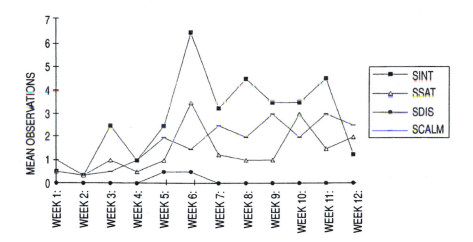

FIGURE 5. Mean Observations of Elder Verbal Academic/Social Behaviors

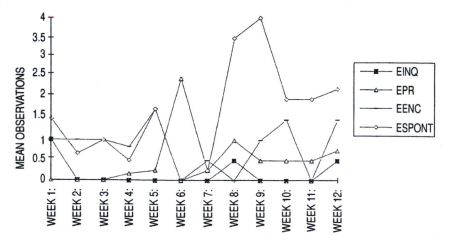

FIGURE 6. Mean Observations of Student Verbal Academic/Social Behaviors

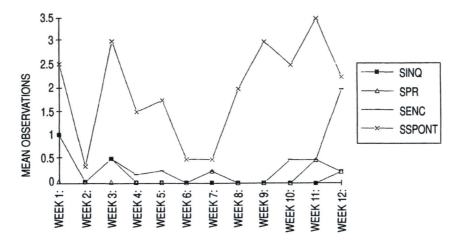

FIGURE 7. Mean Observations of Elder Nonverbal Academic/Social Behaviors

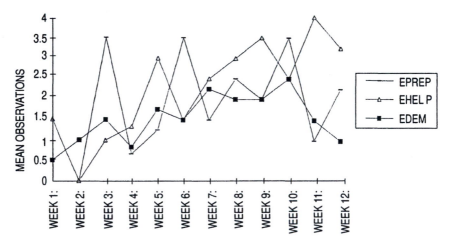

FIGURE 8. Mean Observations of Student Nonverbal Academic/Social Behaviors

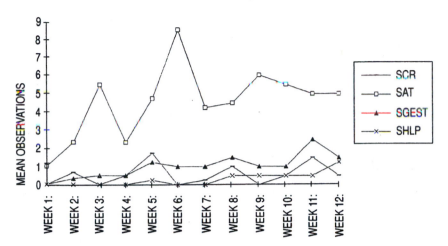

FIGURE 9. Mean Observations of Elder Nonverbal Academic/Social Behaviors

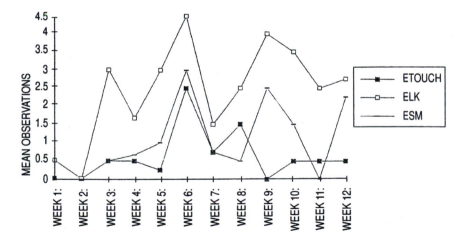

FIGURE 10. Mean Observations of Student Nonverbal Academic/Social Behaviors

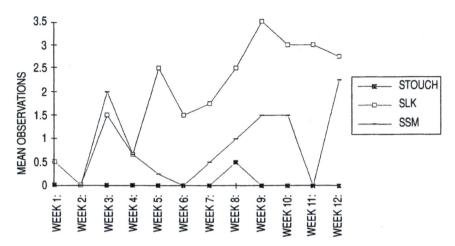

FIGURE 11. Mean Frequency of Observations During Craft and Growing Activities

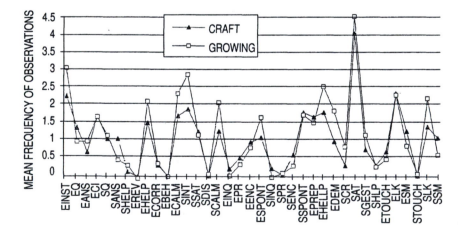

CONCLUSIONS

These data that establishing relationships takes time and depends on opportunities for interaction. Based on the data collected and the subjective opinions of the observers, increased companionship developed in most of the pairings.

This study suggests that for this study group gardening-related activities are more conducive to intergenerational interaction than craft-type activities. This may be a result of the time of day in which the program took place. The students were anxious for gross motor activity after a full day in school. Living organisms generated more interest than did dried plant material. Planning activities that engaged thinking processes and focused on the garden were very popular and resulted in greater numbers of observed interactions.

The recorders also were able to identify key factors that should be included in planning horticultural therapeutic programs based on interaction between participants. The most critical was that whenever a facilitator intervened in the activity, interaction between the elder-student pair was interrupted. Therefore, if the goal is to increase interaction between participants, the staff must consider the importance of the process over the physical product of the activity and base the decision to interrupt on this criterion.

Thorough planning of each activity becomes a critical factor in the program. Written lesson plans guided the activities. Additional planning became necessary when it was observed that the simple act of handing out materials for the project disrupted interaction between elder and student. An alternative that reduced this type of disruption was to provide each pair with a box. All of the materials needed for the activity were in each box prior to the beginning of the activity. This resulted in more sustained interactions between elder and student.

The elders and students were part of the planning process and therefore understood the role that they were to fulfill. Knowledge of what the program is about and its goals guided participants' behavior. GGNC staff occasionally reminded students and elders of their agreed upon roles. Playing and excessive student-to-student and elder-to-elder talking were discouraged and inappropriate behavior immediately stopped by staff.

Much was learned from this study. Perhaps the most important lesson was the benefit of using observers who can share with facilitators what they see happening during an activity. The study provided guidance for future research that will be invaluable to intergenerational work in horticulture programming.

AHTA Survey of Programs
for Older Adults

Organization: American Association of Homes and Services for the Aging
901 E Street, NW, Suite 500
Washington, DC 20004-2037
USA
202-783-2242
(Fax) 202-783-2255

Contact: Ms. Mary Kemper
Public Relations Specialist

Services provided: The American Association of Homes and Services for the Aging (AAHSA) represents not-for-profit organizations dedicated to providing high-quality health care, housing and services to the nation's elderly. Its membership consists of close to 5000 not-for-profit nursing homes, continuing care retirement communities, senior housing facilities, assisted living and community services. AAHSA organizations serve more than one million older persons of all income levels, creeds and races.

AAHSA serves its members by representing the concerns of not-for-profit organizations that serve the elderly through interaction with Congress and federal agencies. It also strives to enhance the professionalism of practitioners and facilities through the Certification Program for Retirement Housing Professionals, the Continuing Care Accreditation Commission, conferences and programs offered by the AAHSA Professional Development Institute, and publications representing current thinking in the long-term care and retirement housing fields

Institution type: No response
Program type: No response
Population served: No response

[Haworth co-indexing entry note]: "AHTA Survey of Programs for Older Adults." Wells, Suzanne E. Co-published simultaneously in *Activities, Adaptation & Aging* (The Haworth Press, Inc.) Vol. 22, No. 3, 1997, pp. 155-195; and: *Horticultural Therapy and the Older Adult Population* (ed: Suzanne E. Wells) The Haworth Press, Inc., 1997, pp. 155-195. Single or multiple copies of this article are available for a fee from The Haworth Document Delivery Service [1-800-342-9678, 9:00 a.m. - 5:00 p.m. (EST). E-mail address: getinfo@haworth.com].

Special populations served: No response
Is there currently an HT program? No response
When did the program begin? No response
Number of clients per year: No response
Number of clients per group: No response
Indoor/Outdoor? No response
Equipment used: No response
Activities: No response
Do participants sell horticultural products? No response
Who is responsible for the horticultural therapy program? No response
Who staffs the horticultural therapy program? No response
Number of staff: No response
Do you provide inservices/staff development? No response
Are horticultural activities prescribed as a specific therapy? No response
What are other means of enrolling in the program? No response
What aspects of the program do you assess? No response
How is your program funded? No response

*   *   *

Organization: Anita Lynne Home, Inc.
13757 Broadfording Church Road
Hagerstown, MD 21740
USA
301-791-0011
(Fax) 301-791-0018

Contact: Ms. Susan Mott
Program Director

Services provided: Anita Lynne is a residence and day program for adults with developmental disabilities. We provide sheltered workshops, on-and off-campus crew work, residential active living, horticultural therapy, music therapy and physical therapy for those in need. We are also in the process of building an indoor riding ring for horsemanship therapy and animal husbandry
Institution type: Domiciliary care facility with day program
Program type: Private, non-profit
Population served: Adults (22-59)
Special populations served: Mental retardation, physical disabilities, and blindness

Is there currently an HT program? No
When did the program begin? 1994
Number of clients per year: 30
Number of clients per group: 5-6
Indoor/Outdoor? Both, year-round
Equipment used: Light carts, containers and greenhouse
Activities: Vegetable gardening, herbs, crafts, indoor plants, annuals and perennials
Do participants sell horticultural products? Yes
Who is responsible for the horticultural therapy program? Program Director
Who staffs the horticultural therapy program? Grounds Maintenance Crew Leader
Number of staff: 8
Do you provide inservices/staff development? No
Are horticultural activities prescribed as a specific therapy? No
What are other means of enrolling in the program? None at this time
What aspects of the program do you assess? Participant satisfaction and skill development
How is your program funded? Fund-raising events, donations/gifts, sale of products and private donations

* * *

Organization: Asbury Heights
700 Bower Hill Road
Pittsburgh, PA 15243
USA
412-571-5123

Contact: Ms. Joanne H. McDonald, HTR
Horticultural Therapist

Services provided: Therapeutic program for older adults in a retirement community. Population consists of frail elderly in skilled nursing units with varied physical and mental disabilities and independent/apartment/townhouse dwellers. Program designed for groups and individuals using outside garden areas and indoor sites
Institution type: Continuing care retirement community
Program type: Public, non-profit
Population served: Older adults

Special populations served: Physical disabilities, psychiatric disorders, blindness and hearing impairments

Is there currently an HT program? Yes. Therapeutic horticultural therapy program for groups and individuals, including health center, personal care and independent residents.

When did the program begin? 1985

Number of clients per year: 50-100

Number of clients per group: 6-8

Indoor/Outdoor? Both, year-round

Equipment used: Light carts, adaptive tools, raised beds, containers. Designed a horticultural therapy area in the activity center

Activities: Vegetable gardening, herbs, crafts, indoor plants, annuals, perennials, landscape maintenance (for residential garden areas) and landscape installation

Do participants sell horticultural products? Yes

Who is responsible for the horticultural therapy program? Horticultural Therapist

Who staffs the horticultural therapy program? Horticultural Therapist and infrequent volunteers

Number of staff: 1

Do you provide inservices/staff development? No

Are horticultural activities prescribed as a specific therapy? Yes

What are other means of enrolling in the program? Any independent personal care or health center resident may individually select a horticultural therapy activity

What aspects of the program do you assess? Participant satisfaction, therapeutic progress, skill development, work quality index, attendance and knowledge of horticulture

How is your program funded? Parent institution, foundation grants, donations/gifts and private donations

* * *

Organization: Beverly Farm Foundation
6133 Humburt Road
Godfrey, IL
USA
618-466-1187

Contact: Mr. Mark E. Smith
Horticultural Therapist

Services provided: Adult residential ICF/DD/MR facility, Illinois' largest private not-for-profit facility, with 409 beds. The Horticultural Therapy Department is a sub-department of Residential Services

Institution type: Residential facility

Program type: Private, non-profit

Population served: Adults and older adults

Special populations served: Mental retardation, physical disabilities, psychiatric disorders, blindness, hearing impairments and multi-handicapped

Is there currently an HT program? Yes. Clinical setting–focus on active treatment and vocational training

When did the program begin? 1991

Number of clients per year: 345

Number of clients per group: 10

Indoor/Outdoor? Both, year-round

Equipment used: Adaptive tools, raised beds, containers and greenhouse

Activities: Vegetable gardening, fruit orchards, herbs, crafts, indoor plants, annuals, perennials, landscape maintenance and landscape installation

Do participants sell horticultural products? Yes

Who is responsible for the horticultural therapy program? Horticultural Therapist

Who staffs the horticultural therapy program? Horticultural Therapist and aides

Number of staff: 3

Do you provide inservices/staff development? Yes

Are horticultural activities prescribed as a specific therapy? Yes

What are other means of enrolling in the program? Specific evaluation tools for specific individual deficits

What aspects of the program do you assess? Participant satisfaction, therapeutic progress, skill development, work quality index and knowledge of horticulture

How is your program funded? Parent institution, foundation grants, fund raising events, donations/gifts, sale of products and private donations

* * *

Organization: Brandywine Nursing Home
620 Sleepy Hollow Road
Briarcliff Manor, NY 10510
USA
914-941-5100
(Fax) 914-941-4752

Contact: Mr. Paul Roth
                Administrator

Services provided: Nursing home facility offering care for older adults and people in need of rehabilitation and full time care.
Institution type: Nursing home
Program type: Public, for profit
Population served: Adults and older adults
Special populations served: Mental retardation, physical disabilities, psychiatric disorders, blindness and hearing impairments
Is there currently an HT program? No response.
When did the program begin? No response
Number of clients per year: No response
Number of clients per group: No response
Indoor/Outdoor? No response
Equipment used: No response
Activities: No response
Do participants sell horticultural products? No response
Who is responsible for the horticultural therapy program? Horticultural Therapy
Who staffs the horticultural therapy program? Horticultural Therapist, Recreational Therapist, and volunteer
Number of staff: 1
Do you provide inservices/staff development? Yes
Are horticultural activities prescribed as a specific therapy? No
What are other means of enrolling in the program? Based on comprehensive care plan assessments and resident interest
What aspects of the program do you assess? Participant satisfaction, therapeutic progress, skill development, attendance and quality assurance audits
How is your program funded? No response

                          *   *   *

Organization: CareWest
                1070 McDougall Road, NE
                Calgary, Alberta, T2E 7Z2
                Canada
                403-267-2900 or 403-686-8121
                (Fax) 403-686-8104

Contact: Mr. Chris Makin
                Coordinator, Horticultural Services

Services provided: Provides housing care, hospitality and rehab services for five long-term care centres, day hospital services, psychogeriatric counseling, placement
Institution type: Nursing home
Program type: Private, non-profit
Population served: Adults and older adults
Special populations served: Physical disabilities and psychiatric disorders
Is there currently an HT program? Yes
When did the program begin? 1984
Number of clients per year: 200
Number of clients per group: 3 to 8
Indoor/Outdoor? Both, year-round
Equipment used: Light carts, adaptive tools, raised beds, containers, greenhouse and window sills (sunrooms)
Activities: Vegetable gardening, herbs, indoor plants, annuals and perennials
Do participants sell horticultural products? Yes
Who is responsible for the horticultural therapy program? Recreational Therapist
Who staffs the horticultural therapy program? Horticultural Therapist, Recreational Therapist and volunteer
Number of staff: 14
Do you provide inservices/staff development? Yes
Are horticultural activities prescribed as a specific therapy? Yes
What are other means of enrolling in the program? General interest
What aspects of the program do you assess? Participant satisfaction, therapeutic progress and attendance
How is your program funded? Parent institution, donations/gifts, sale of products and private donations

* * *

Organization: Cheyenne Botanic Gardens
710 South Lions Park Drive
Cheyenne, WY 82001
USA
307-637-6458
(Fax) 307-637-6459

Contact: Mr. Shane Smith
Director

Services provided: Senior, youth and disabled volunteers provide the main labor force for the Cheyenne Botanic Gardens. We also function as a municipal nursery, as well as providing education, food and therapy. The conservatory is 100% solar heated

Institution type: Botanic garden
Program type: Public, non-profit
Population served: Adolescents, adults and older adults
Special populations served: Mental retardation, physical disabilities, psychiatric disorders, blindness, and hearing impairments
Is there currently an HT program? Yes
When did the program begin? 1976
Number of clients per year: 80-100
Number of clients per group: 15-50
Indoor/Outdoor? Both, year-round
Equipment used: Adaptive tools, raised beds, containers and greenhouse
Activities: Vegetable gardening, fruit orchards, herbs, crafts, indoor plants, annuals, perennials, landscape maintenance and landscape installation
Do participants sell horticultural products? No
Who is responsible for the horticultural therapy program? Horticultural Therapist
Who staffs the horticultural therapy program? Horticultural Therapist and volunteer
Number of staff: 3
Do you provide inservices/staff development? No
Are horticultural activities prescribed as a specific therapy? Yes
What are other means of enrolling in the program? Retired Senior Volunteer Program, Green Thumb Program and Southeast Mental Health Center
What aspects of the program do you assess? Participant satisfaction, therapeutic progress, skill development, attendance and knowledge of horticulture
How is your program funded? Parent institution, government grants, foundation grants, fund raising events, donations/gifts and private donations

* * *

Organization: Crafts-Farrow State Hospital
7901 Farrow Road
Columbia, SC 29203
USA
803-935-6887

Contact: Ms. Liz Fuller
Director of Horticultural Therapy

Services provided: CFHS provides treatment services for the geriatric, psychiatric population CFSH Horticultural Therapy
Institution type: Psychiatric institution
Program type: Public, non-profit
Population served: Older adults
Special populations served: Psychiatric disorders
Is there currently an HT program? Yes. Greenhouse and gardening horticulture therapy program for geriatric psychiatric adults
When did the program begin? 1980
Number of clients per year: 85
Number of clients per group: 4-6
Indoor/Outdoor?: Both, year-round
Equipment used: Light carts, raised beds, containers and greenhouse
Activities: Vegetable gardening, herbs, crafts, indoor plants, annuals, perennials, landscape maintenance and landscape installation
Do participants sell horticultural products? Yes
Who is responsible for the horticultural therapy program? Horticultural Therapist
Who staffs the horticultural therapy program? Horticultural Therapist, volunteer and aides
Number of staff: 2
Do you provide inservices/staff development? Yes
Are horticultural activities prescribed as a specific therapy? Yes
What are other means of enrolling in the program? All patients are referred by the treatment team
What aspects of the program do you assess? Participant satisfaction, therapeutic progress and skill development
How is your program funded? Parent institution and sale of products

*   *   *

Organization: The Companion Gardener, Inc.
                            9857 SW 117 Court
                            Miami, FL 33186-2755
                            USA
                            305-274-2774

Contact: Ms. Alee Karpf
                     Director of Clinical Services

Services provided: Psychotherapy utilizing plants and related materials as stimuli in the therapeutic process; specifically working with frail older adults. This program is particularly helpful with patients who have become withdrawn, depressed, are grieving, have diminished self-esteem, are nonverbal or demonstrating isolating behavior

Institution type: Nursing home
Program type: Public, for profit
Population served: Older adults (ages 60 and over)
Special populations served: No response
Is there currently an HT program? Yes. Utilize growth and care of plants and related plant activities to stimulate psychotherapeutic process in group as well as individual settings
When did the program begin? 1994
Number of clients per year: 30-35
Number of clients per group: 3-5
Indoor/Outdoor? Both, year-round
Equipment used: Light carts, adaptive tools, and containers
Activities: Herbs, crafts, indoor plants and annuals
Do participants sell horticultural products? No
Who is responsible for the horticultural therapy program? No response
Who staffs the horticultural therapy program? No response
Number of staff: No response
Do you provide inservices/staff development? No response
Are horticultural activities prescribed as a specific therapy? No response
What are other means of enrolling in the program? No response
What aspects of the program do you assess? No response
How is your program funded? Insurance for psychotherapy services

* * *

Organization: Dr. Yeager Health Center
Sanitorium Road
Pomona, NY 10970
USA
914-364-2000

Contact: Ms. Marianne Riccaldo
Director of Rehabilitation

Services provided: Rehabilitation services include: occupational therapy, physical therapy, speech and horticultural therapy
Institution type: Nursing home
Program type: Public, non-profit
Population served: Adults and older adults

Special populations served: Physical disabilities, blindness and hearing impairments

Is there currently an HT program? Yes. Part of the Occupational Therapy Department using specific goals therapeutically with 20 patients weekly. Using plants to accomplish these goals: strengthening, endurance, R.O.M., dexterity, fine and gross motor skills and coordination.

When did the program begin? 1980

Number of clients per year: 50

Number of clients per group: 4-6

Indoor/Outdoor? Both, year-round

Equipment used: Light carts, adaptive tools, raised beds, containers and greenhouse

Activities: Vegetable gardening, herbs, crafts, indoor plants, annuals and house plants

Do participants sell horticultural products? Yes

Who is responsible for the horticultural therapy program? Occupational Therapist

Who staffs the horticultural therapy program? Occupational Therapist and Director of Rehabilitation

Number of staff: 1

Do you provide inservices/staff development? Yes

Are horticultural activities prescribed as a specific therapy? Yes

What are other means of enrolling in the program? As a recreational activity—one session per week

What aspects of the program do you assess? Participant satisfaction, therapeutic progress, skill development, work quality index, attendance and therapeutic goals met

How is your program funded? Parent institution and sale of products

*   *   *

Organization: Eastern State Hospital
4601 Ironbound Road
P.O. Box 8791
Williamsburg, VA 23187-8791
USA
804-253-5392
(Fax) 804-253-5192

Contact: Ms. Betty G. Jones
Human Service Care Specialist

Services provided: Horticultural Therapy program
Institution type: Psychiatric institution
Program type: Public, non-profit
Population served: Adults and older adults
Special populations served: Mental retardation, addictive disorders and psychiatric disorders
Is there currently an HT program? Yes. Classes in plant care, maintenance, propagation, plant crafts, and gardening are organized to fit the mental/physical conditions of our patients.
When did the program begin? 1982
Number of clients per year: 220+
Number of clients per group: 4-8
Indoor/Outdoor? Both, year-round
Equipment used: Light carts, adaptive tools, raised beds, containers, greenhouse and former automotive workshop for garden workshop. Glassed, paned baydoor for a mini-greenhouse effect.
Activities: Vegetable gardening, herbs, crafts, indoor plants, annuals, perennials, landscape maintenance and landscape installation (small scale)
Do participants sell horticultural products? Yes
Who is responsible for the horticultural therapy program? Horticultural Therapist
Who staffs the horticultural therapy program? Horticultural Therapist
Number of staff: 1
Do you provide inservices/staff development? Yes
Are horticultural activities prescribed as a specific therapy? Yes
What are other means of enrolling in the program? Treatment team may assign patients; but patients can opt for program as well
What aspects of the program do you assess? Participant satisfaction, therapeutic progress, skill development, work quality index and attendance
How is your program funded? Donations/gifts, sale of products and from hospital budget

*   *   *

Organization: Forest Trace at Inverrary
5500 NW 69th Avenue
Lauderhill, FL 33319
USA
305-572-1800

Contact: Mr. Robert Bornstein, HTR
Garden Club Horticultural Therapist

Services provided: Provide quality horticulture related activities weekly to an independent adult congregate living facility. Groups include plant clinics and propagation, vegetable and flower gardens in containers, flowers, herbs, nature walks, crafts and much more. Garden Club
Institution type: Retirement center
Program type: Private, for profit
Population served: Older adults
Special populations served: Physical disabilities, hearing impairments and slight dementia
Is there currently an HT program? Yes. Weekly sessions covering a wide variety of horticulture practices, mostly "hands on" activities, also have a container vegetable garden
When did the program begin? 1995
Number of clients per year: 780
Number of clients per group: 12-18
Indoor/Outdoor? Both, year-round
Equipment used: Adaptive tools, raised beds and containers
Activities: Vegetable gardening, herbs, crafts, indoor plants, annuals, perennials and nature trails
Do participants sell horticultural products? No
Who is responsible for the horticultural therapy program? Horicultural Therapist
Who staffs the horticultural therapy program? Horticultural Therapist
Number of staff: 1
Do you provide inservices/staff development? Yes
Are horticultural activities prescribed as a specific therapy? No
What are other means of enrolling in the program? Voluntary program
What aspects of the program do you assess? Participant satisfaction and attendance
How is your program funded? Residents pay set fee for all services provided. Horticultural therapy budget comes from activity director budget

* * *

Organization: Green Eacker's Vocational Training Program
P.O. Box 972/ 3 Butternut Drive
Pelham, NH 03076-0972
USA
603-635-3631

Contact: Ms. Loretta Eacker
Occupational Therapy Aide/ Sole Proprietor

Services provided: Living adult skills; essential life needs; leisure programs; gross motor and fine motor skills through plant care, gardening, etc., adaptive equipment at Tyngsboro Group Home
Institution type: Adult living home
Program type: Public, non-profit
Population served: Adults and older adults
Special populations served: Mental retardation, physical disabilities, psychiatric disorders and blindness
Is there currently an HT program? Yes. Care for house plants; hanging basket gardening. Limited due to clients' age.
When did the program begin? 1993
Number of clients per year: 8
Number of clients per group: 2-3
Indoor/Outdoor? Both, year-round
Equipment used: Adaptive tools and containers
Activities: Crafts, indoor plants and annuals
Do participants sell horticultural products? No
Who is responsible for the horticultural therapy program? Occupational aide
Who staffs the horticultural therapy program? Occupational Aide and residential staff
Number of staff: 4
Do you provide inservices/staff development? Yes
Are horticultural activities prescribed as a specific therapy? Yes
What are other means of enrolling in the program? Horticultural therapy used as a tool to work with fine and gross motor skills; physical therapy and occupational therapy
What aspects of the program do you assess? Participant satisfaction and attendance
How is your program funded? Government grants/state funding

* * *

Organization: Green Thumb, Inc.
2000 North 14th Street, Suite 800
Arlington, VA 22201
USA
703-522-7272
(Fax) 703-522-0141

Contact: Ms. Helen Ericson
Asst. to the Pres. for Communications

Services provided: Green Thumb, Inc. provides employment and training services for Older Americans under Title V (the Senior Community Service Employment Program) of the Older Americans Act and Job Training Partnership Act in 44 states and Puerto Rico. Participants are 55 years of age or older and have limited income. Green Thumb pays participants the minimum wage for approximately 20 hours of community service each week while they receive training, work experience, and supportive services designed to prepare them for employment

Institution type: No response
Program type: No response
Population served: No response
Special populations served: No response
Is there currently an HT program? No response
When did the program begin? No response
Number of clients per year: No response
Number of clients per group: No response
Indoor/Outdoor? No response
Equipment used: No response
Activities: No response
Do participants sell horticultural products? No response
Who is responsible for the horticultural therapy program? No response
Who staffs the horticultural therapy program? No response
Number of staff: No response
Do you provide inservices/staff development? No response
Are horticultural activities prescribed as a specific therapy? No response
What are other means of enrolling in the program? No response
What aspects of the program do you assess? No response
How is your program funded? No response

* * *

Organization: Harmony House Health Care Center
2950 West Shaulis Road
Waterloo, IA 50701
USA
319-234-4495 extension 51
(Fax) 319-236-1831

Contact: Ms. Kelly Jane Conrad, HTT
Horticultural Therapist

Services provided: We offer quality of life to any individual with an interest in horticulture activities, utilizing a 3000 square foot greenhouse, 14

flower beds and 1 vegetable garden. We enhance daily routines with this non-threatening environment. Harmony House Greenhouse

Institution type: Nursing home

Program type: Private, for profit

Population served: Adolescents, adults and older adults

Special populations served: Mental retardation, physical disabilities, addictive disorders, psychiatric disorders, blindness, hearing impairments and head injuries

Is there currently an HT program? Yes. We have 92 residents scheduled every week for at least 30 minutes up to 20 hours per week

When did the program begin? 1993

Number of clients per year: 100

Number of clients per group: 1-4

Indoor/Outdoor? Both, year-round

Equipment used: Adaptive tools, raised beds, containers and greenhouse

Activities: Vegetable gardening, herbs, crafts, indoor plants, annuals, perennials, landscape maintenance, landscape installation, nature trails and equipment care

Do participants sell horticultural products? Yes

Who is responsible for the horticultural therapy program? Horticultural Therapist

Who staffs the horticultural therapy program? Horticultural Therapist

Number of staff: 2

Do you provide inservices/staff development? Yes

Are horticultural activities prescribed as a specific therapy? Yes

What are other means of enrolling in the program? Same-day programming for other people for job or basic training (volunteers)

What aspects of the program do you assess? Participant satisfaction, therapeutic progress, skill development, work quality index, attendance and knowledge of horticulture

How is your program funded? Parent institution and sale of products

* * *

Organization: HealthSouth RIOSA
9119 Cinnamon Hill
San Antonio, TX 78240
USA
800-688-0737
(Fax) 210-558-1297

Contact: Ms. Lyn Saunders
Director of Therapeutic Recreation

Services provided: This therapeutic garden program is unique in that it is directed by the Therapeutic Recreation Department and all therapy is done in conjunction with physical therapists. It's a year-round program focusing on rehabilitation goals of a physical, cognitive and social nature. We have an outdoor raised bed garden at various heights and use adaptive tools. We have several fun annual/seasonal events to market ourselves and raise money

Institution type: Rehabilitation hospital

Program type: Public, for profit

Population served: Adolescents (13-21), adults (22-59) and older adults (60+)

Special populations served: Physical disabilities, blindness, hearing impairments and burn survivors

Is there currently an HT program? Yes. Enabling garden–outdoor adaptive tools, nature crafts, cooking and special events/sales, physical therapy assists therapeutic recreation department and group

When did the program begin? 1991

Number of clients per year: 300

Number of clients per group: 8-14

Indoor/Outdoor? Both, year-round

Equipment used: Light carts, adaptive tools, raised beds, containers and vertical gardens

Activities: Vegetable gardening, herbs, crafts, annuals, perennials and landscape maintenance

Do participants sell horticultural products? Yes

Who is responsible for the horticultural therapy program? Recreational Therapist

Who staffs the horticultural therapy program? Recreational Therapist and Physical Therapist

Number of staff: 4

Do you provide inservices/staff development? Yes

Are horticultural activities prescribed as a specific therapy? Yes

What are other means of enrolling in the program? Referral by physician, treatment team or family or interest of patient

What aspects of the program do you assess? Participant satisfaction, therapeutic progress, skill development

How is your program funded? Parent institution

* * *

Organization: Heather Farm Garden Center
1540 Marenbanks Drive
Walnut Creek, LA 94598
USA
510-947-6712 or 510-706-8387

Contact: Ms. Tina Mraz
Horticultural Therapy Director

Services provided: A Horticultural Therapy program meets twice per month. Participants come to us from retirement and convalescent homes and Alzheimer's facilities. We will soon be adding raised beds which are wheelchair accessible so participants can actually "garden" in our program. Currently we do nature and plant related crafts and start and propagate plants in pots
Institution type: Arboretum/garden center
Program type: Public, non-profit
Population served: Adolescents, adults and older adults
Special populations served: Mental retardation, physical disabilities, addictive disorders, psychiatric disorders, blindness and hearing impairments. Anyone is welcome
Is there currently an HT program? Yes. We meet 2 times per month for 1-1/2 hours each and do planting in containers and plant related crafts. Participant also enjoy our demonstration gardens
When did the program begin? 1987
Number of clients per year: 500
Number of clients per group: 25
Indoor/Outdoor? Both, year-round
Equipment used: Raised beds (in the future) and containers
Activities: Herbs, crafts, indoor plants, annuals and nature trails in our garden
Do participants sell horticultural products? No
Who is responsible for the horticultural therapy program? Horticultural Therapist
Who staffs the horticultural therapy program? Horticultural Therapist, volunteer and aides
Number of staff: 4-6
Do you provide inservices/staff development? No
Are horticultural activities prescribed as a specific therapy? No

What are other means of enrolling in the program? Open to the community–anyone may come
What aspects of the program do you assess? Participant satisfaction and information from activity directors from different facilities
How is your program funded? Foundation grants, fund raising events, donations/gifts and other: $2.00 participation fee

*   *   *

Organization: Homewood Health Centre
                    Horticultural Therapy Department
                    150 Delhi Street
                    Guelph, Ontario, NIE 6K9
                    Canada
                    519-824-1010 extension 180
                    (Fax) 519-822-6619

Contact: Mr. Mitchell Hewson, HTM
                    Director of Horticultural Therapy Department

Services provided: Horticultural therapy program provides specialized treatment for clients over 65 with depression or dementia; for clients of all ages with affective disorders, substance abuse and eating disorders. Classes are conducted with each group using horticulture or horticulturally related crafts as a tool to develop a therapeutic relationship and teach viable skills that can be used upon discharge. Geropsychiatry service–Horticultural therapy
Institution type: Psychiatric institution
Program type: Private, for profit
Population served: Adults and older adults
Special populations served: Physical disabilities, addictive disorders, psychiatric disorders and other: dementia, depression (65+) and eating disorders
Is there currently an HT program? Yes. Longest running and largest horticultural therapy program in Canada. Private psychiatric hospital specializes in the treatment of dementia and depression (over 65), affective disorders, substance abuse and eating disorders
When did the program begin? 1974
Number of clients per year: 2600
Number of clients per group: 8
Indoor/Outdoor? Both, year-round
Equipment used: Light carts, adaptive tools, raised beds, containers and greenhouse

Activities: Vegetable gardening, herbs, crafts, indoor plants, annuals, perennials, landscape maintenance, landscape installation and nature trails
Do participants sell horticultural products? No
Who is responsible for the horticultural therapy program? Horticultural Therapist
Who staffs the horticultural therapy program? Horticultural Therapist and volunteer
Number of staff: 2
Do you provide inservices/staff development? Yes
Are horticultural activities prescribed as a specific therapy? Yes
What are other means of enrolling in the program? Optional activity for depressed and dementia population (four times per week) and geropsychiatry service
What aspects of the program do you assess? Participant satisfaction, rate of recovery, length of hospital stay, therapeutic progress, skill development, work quality index, attendance and knowledge of horticulture
How is your program funded? Parent institution and sale of products

* * *

Organization: Horticultural Therapy Services
Chicago Botanic Garden
P.O. Box 400
Glencoe, IL 60022
USA
708-835-8248
(Fax) 708-835-1635

Contact: Mr. Matthew Frazel, HTR
Supervisor

Services provided: Horticultural Therapy Services provides outreach training programs to health care and human service facilities throughout the Chicago area. Our focus is on staff training. We aim to teach how to use gardening (indoor and outdoor) to staff from a wide variety of facilities. We also maintain a demonstration Enabling Garden on grounds of the Botanic Garden. In addition, we act as an information clearinghouse for ideas related to horticultural therapy
Institution type: Arboretum/garden center
Program type: Private, non-profit
Population served: Children (12 and under), adolescents (13-21) adults (22-59) and older adults (60+)

Special populations served: Mental retardation, physical disabilities, addictive disorders, psychiatric disorders, blindness, hearing impairments and corrections

Is there currently an HT program? Yes. Outreach contract services to social service agencies, providing horticultural therapy training to staff. Curate the Enabling Garden for People with Disabilities, information clearinghouse

When did the program begin? 1978

Number of clients per year: 450

Number of clients per group: 15

Indoor/Outdoor? Both, year-round

Equipment used: Light carts, adaptive tools, raised beds, containers and greenhouse

Activities: Vegetable gardening, fruit orchards, herbs, crafts, indoor plants, annuals and perennials

Do participants sell horticultural products? Yes

Who is responsible for the horticultural therapy program? Horticultural/Recreational Therapist

Who staffs the horticultural therapy program? Horticultural Therapist and Recreational Therapist

Number of staff: 2

Do you provide inservices/staff development? Yes

Are horticultural activities prescribed as a specific therapy? Sometimes

What are other means of enrolling in the program? Classroom enrollment

What aspects of the program do you assess? Participant satisfaction

How is your program funded? Parent institution and fees for service

* * *

Organization: Ida Culver House Broadview
12505 Greenwood Avenue, N
Seattle, WA 98133
USA
206-361-1989
(Fax) 206-368-3757

Contact: Ms. Sheila B. Taft, HTR
Horticultural Therapist

Services provided: Retirement community offering independent and assisted living and skilled nursing facility. Skilled nursing offers three programs: cognitive impairment; residential; and rehabilitation. Developed in

conjunction with Seattle Education Auxiliary and University of Washington School of Nursing
Institution type: Nursing home
Program type: Public, for profit
Population served: Older adults
Special populations served: Physical disabilities and cognitive impairment
Is there currently an HT program? Yes. Two group sessions per week and one-on-one program. Two outdoor gardens with raised beds, as well as balcony planters and indoor planters.
When did the program begin? 1991
Number of clients per year: 40
Number of clients per group: 7-12
Indoor/Outdoor? Both, year-round
Equipment used: Light carts, adaptive tools, raised beds and containers
Activities: Vegetable gardening, herbs, crafts, indoor plants, annuals and perennials
Do participants sell horticultural products? No
Who is responsible for the horticultural therapy program? Horticultural Therapist
Who staffs the horticultural therapy program? Horticultural Therapist and volunteer
Number of staff: 1
Do you provide inservices/staff development? No
Are horticultural activities prescribed as a specific therapy? No
What are other means of enrolling in the program? Voluntary participation as part of facility's activity program
What aspects of the program do you assess? Participant satisfaction, skill development and attendance
How is your program funded? Parent institution and fund raising events

* * *

Organization: La Vida Felicidad, Inc.
P.O. Box 2040
Los Lunas, NM 87031
USA
505-865-4651
(Fax) 505-865-5331

Contact: Ms. Bernardine Baca Spiers, HTT
Adult Day Care Coordinator

Services provided: Family-centered intervention for people with special needs providing adult daycare for the disabled, homemaker services, respite, early intervention for children (birth-3) and adult activity program

Institution type: Other
Program type: Private, non-profit
Population served: Children (12 and under), adults and older adults
Special populations served: Mental retardation, physical disabilities, psychiatric disorders, hearing impairments and stroke
Is there currently an HT program? Yes. Greenhouse, raised beds and containers. One taken care of by participants with a variety of disabilities
When did the program begin? 1994
Number of clients per year: 17
Number of clients per group: 10
Indoor/Outdoor? Both, year-round
Equipment used: Light carts, adaptive tools, raised beds, containers and greenhouse
Activities: Vegetable gardening, herbs, crafts, indoor plants, annuals, perennials, landscape maintenance, landscape installation
Do participants sell horticultural products? No
Who is responsible for the horticultural therapy program? Horticultural Therapist
Who staffs the horticultural therapy program? Horticultural Therapist and aides
Number of staff: 3
Do you provide inservices/staff development? Yes
Are horticultural activities prescribed as a specific therapy? Yes
What are other means of enrolling in the program? No response
What aspects of the program do you assess? Participant satisfaction, therapeutic progress, skill development and attendance
How is your program funded? Government grants and fund-raising events

* * *

Organization: Legacy Health System/Legacy Portland Hospital
2430 NW Marshall
Portland, OR 97210
USA
503-227-3791
(Fax) 503-248-0855

Contact: Ms. Teresia Hazen, HTR
Horticultural Therapist

Services provided: The two downtown hospitals provide horticultural therapy services through Legacy Rehabilitation Services. HT services are provided at each Skilled Nursing Facility and Pediatrics (Legacy Emanual Children's Hospital). Each site offers indoor programming as well as outdoor gardens. Legacy Good Samaritan Hospital HT/OT/PT/RT are developing plans for a botanical garden and garden for rehabilitation

Institution type: Rehabilitation hospital
Program type: Public, non-profit
Population served: Children, adolescents, adults and older adults
Special populations served: Mental retardation, physical disabilities, addictive disorders, psychiatric disorders, blindness and hearing impairments
Is there currently an HT program? Yes. Treatment groups and individual sessions at two Skilled Nursing Facilities and groups for Pediatric Acute and Rehabilitation
When did the program begin? 1991
Number of clients per year: 300
Number of clients per group: 5
Indoor/Outdoor? Both, year-round
Equipment used: Light carts, adaptive tools, raised beds and containers
Activities: Herbs, crafts, indoor plants, annuals and perennials
Do participants sell horticultural products? Yes
Who is responsible for the horticultural therapy program? Horticultural Therapist
Who staffs the horticultural therapy program? Horticultural Therapist, O.T., P.T., S.L.P. and volunteer
Number of staff: 4
Do you provide inservices/staff development? Yes
Are horticultural activities prescribed as a specific therapy? Yes
What are other means of enrolling in the program? No response
What aspects of the program do you assess? Participant satisfaction, rate of recovery, length of hospital stay, therapeutic progress and skill development
How is your program funded? Parent institution, fund raising events, donations/gifts, sale of products and private donations

* * *

Organization: The Lodge of Montgomery
                    12050 Montgomery Road
                    Cincinnati, OH 45249
                    USA
                    513-683-9966

Contact: Ms. Melanie Trelaine
                    Activity Director

Services provided: Weekly horticultural therapy programs for elderly residents—most physically or visually handicapped. Residents are independent and have patios to grow outdoor container gardens as well as houseplants. Therapeutic activities are necessary for residents in assisted living wings. We have just completed raised beds outside

Institution type: Retirement center
Program type: Public, for profit
Population served: Older adults
Special populations served: Physical disabilities, blindness and hearing impairments
Is there currently an HT program? Yes. Weekly programs covering range of topics and interactive activities
When did the program begin? 1994
Number of clients per year: 50
Number of clients per group: 10
Indoor/Outdoor? Both, year-round
Equipment used: Light carts, adaptive tools, raised beds, containers and greenhouse
Activities: Vegetable gardening, herbs, crafts, indoor plants, annuals, perennials, landscape installation and nature trails
Do participants sell horticultural products? Yes
Who is responsible for the horticultural therapy program? Horticultural Therapist
Who staffs the horticultural therapy program? Horticultural Therapist
Number of staff: 1
Do you provide inservices/staff development? No
Are horticultural activities prescribed as a specific therapy? Yes
What are other means of enrolling in the program? Open to all residents
What aspects of the program do you assess? Participant satisfaction, therapeutic progress, skill development, attendance, knowledge of horticulture and peer training
How is your program funded? Parent institution

* * *

Organization: Memorial Hospital
3501 Johnson Street
Hollywood, FL 33021
USA
305-987-2000 extension 5486
(Fax) 305-985-3416

Contact: Mr. Robert Bornstein, HTR
Horticultural Therapist

Services provided: Diverse horticultural therapy program serving seniors, day treatment, admissions, treatment and open units for a psychiatric

section of a hospital (100-bed psychiatric center, part of a community non-profit hospital, work in conjunction with Occupational Therapists, Recreational Therapists and music therapy in adult care setting)
Institution type: Hospital
Program type: Public, non-profit
Population served: Adults and older adults
Special populations served: Mental retardation, physical disabilities, addictive disorders, psychiatric disorders, blindness and hearing impairments
Is there currently an HT program? Yes. A diversified program in a psychiatric hospital setting, with indoor table top activities and patios for container gardening and plant propagation benches
When did the program begin? 1995
Number of clients per year: New N/A
Number of clients per group: 8
Indoor/Outdoor? Both, year-round
Equipment used: Adaptive tools, raised beds, containers, and patios
Activities: Herbs, crafts, indoor plants, annuals and foliage plants
Do participants sell horticultural products? No
Who is responsible for the horticultural therapy program? Horticultural Therapist
Who staffs the horticultural therapy program? Horticultural Therapist
Number of staff: 1
Do you provide inservices/staff development? Yes
Are horticultural activities prescribed as a specific therapy? Yes
What are other means of enrolling in the program? Referral by other therapists, team members
What aspects of the program do you assess? Participant satisfaction, therapeutic progress and attendance
How is your program funded? Hospital special taxing district (taxes paid by homeowners)

*   *   *

Organization: Mental Health Services, Inc.
                   P.O. Box 119
                   Livingston, MT 59047
                   USA
                   406-547-3354

Contact: Ms. Mary Ellen M. Spogis
                   Mental Health Therapist

Services provided: Rural group horticultural therapy to Medicaid recipients within a nursing home located in an extremely rural area

Institution type: Nursing home/community mental health center
Program type: Private, non-profit
Population served: Older adults
Special populations served: Physical disabilities, psychiatric disorders, blindness and hearing impairments
Is there currently an HT program? Yes. Rural groups for elderly
When did the program begin? 1992
Number of clients per year: 7-10
Number of clients per group: 10
Indoor/Outdoor? Both, year-round
Equipment used: Containers
Activities: Vegetable gardening, herbs, crafts, indoor plants
Do participants sell horticultural products? No
Who is responsible for the horticultural therapy program? Horticultural Therapist
Who staffs the horticultural therapy program? Horticultural Therapist, Activity Therapist and aides
Number of staff: 1
Do you provide inservices/staff development? Yes
Are horticultural activities prescribed as a specific therapy? Yes
What are other means of enrolling in the program? Medicaid recipients and willingness to participate
What aspects of the program do you assess? Participant satisfaction, therapeutic progress, skill development, work quality index, attendance and knowledge of horticulture
How is your program funded? Parent institution

*   *   *

Organization: Mercy Center for Health Care Services
1325 North Highland Avenue
Aurora, IL 60506
USA
708-859-2222 extension 2580
(Fax) 708-859-8746

Contact: Ms. Kathleen Mlyniec-Ellmann, CTRS, HTT
Certified Therapeutic Recreation Specialist

Services provided: We offer horticultural therapy once per week to the older adult population. The types of activities vary week to week and may include being out in the courtyard, floral design, nature crafts and planting

Institution type: Hospital
Program type: Public, non-profit
Population served: Children, adolescents, adults and older adults
Special populations served: Mental retardation, physical disabilities, addictive disorders, psychiatric disorders, blindness and hearing impairments
Is there currently an HT program? Yes. Provide Horticulture Therapy once a week to adults and older adults offering a variety of activities, children and adolescents are served approximately once per month
When did the program begin? 1984
Number of clients per year: 2600
Number of clients per group: 10
Indoor/Outdoor? Both, year-round
Equipment used: Light carts, adaptive tools and containers
Activities: Crafts, indoor plants, annuals, perennials, and landscape maintenance
Do participants sell horticultural products? No
Who is responsible for the horticultural therapy program? Recreational Therapist
Who staffs the horticultural therapy program? Horticultural Therapist and Recreational Therapist
Number of staff: 2
Do you provide inservices/staff development? No
Are horticultural activities prescribed as a specific therapy? Yes
What are other means of enrolling in the program? None
What aspects of the program do you assess? Participant satisfaction, therapeutic progress and attendance
How is your program funded? Parent institution and reimbursement

* * *

Organization: Meridian Perring Parkway–Member of the Genesis Health Venture
1801 Wentworth Road
Baltimore, MD 21234
USA
410-661-5717
(Fax) 410-668-4328

Contact: Ms. Dee McGuire, HTT
Assistant Activities Director

Services provided: The interdisciplinary team provides the services that meet our residents needs: 24-hour, 120 bed facility nursing care, medical supervision, group and individual activities, horticultural therapist on staff and special therapeutic diets. Social services provide counseling, discharge referral and placement. The facility offers rehabilitation through the physical therapy and occupational therapy team. Respite (short stay) care is also provided. Consultants are available including a dentist, podiatrist, ophthalmologist, pharmacist and psychiatrist. We are involved with hospitals, churches and the business community. Many outreach programs from various organizations including the Department of Aging are provided, as part of the Activities Program

Institution type: Nursing home

Program type: Public, for profit

Population served: Adults and older adults

Special populations served: Physical disabilities, psychiatric disorders, blindness, hearing impairments, cognitive impairments, Alzheimer's and related dementia, head injury

Is there currently an HT program? Yes. A successful horticultural therapy activity program offered as a modality of treatment through the activities program, which I have promoted and which is part of an interdisciplinary team in this long term care setting. A variety of activities using natural materials in a group or one-to-one setting three to four times a week which offers opportunity for assessment, function levels while establishing goals/ objectives that can be measured. The benefits have extended to staff, volunteers, families and friends

When did the program begin? 1992

Number of clients per year: 120-200

Number of clients per group: 10-15

Indoor/Outdoor? Both, year-round

Equipment used: Light carts, adaptive tools, containers and window sills

Activities: Vegetable gardening, herbs, crafts, indoor plants, annuals, perennials and flower arranging

Do participants sell horticultural products? Yes

Who is responsible for the horticultural therapy program? Horticultural Therapist

Who staffs the horticultural therapy program? Horticultural Therapist, Activity Therapist, volunteer and family members

Number of staff: 1-2

Do you provide inservices/staff development? Yes

Are horticultural activities prescribed as a specific therapy? Yes

What are other means of enrolling in the program? Families encourage residents; individual residents will request self-directed activities; also individual residents will come along to watch but will then begin to actively become engaged; and "repetition" attraction

What aspects of the program do you assess? Participant satisfaction, therapeutic progress, skill development, attendance, knowledge of horticulture, interactive with peers or staff–expressive, reminiscence, and validational results

How is your program funded? Donations/gifts, sale of products and annual budget from Activities Department

* * *

Organization: North Princeton Developmental Center
P.O. Box 1000
Princeton, NJ 08543
USA
609-466-0400 extension 233

Contact: Ms. Devah Brinker, HTR
Teacher I (of Persons with Handicaps)

Services provided: Vocational/educational greenhouse workshop for residential developmentally disabled older adults. Individual task training and outdoor gardens combined with small scale landscaping around residential homes to increase mobility, attitude, mental disposition and longevity without undue deterioration

Institution type: Sheltered workshop and vocational school

Program type: Public, non-profit

Population served: Adults and older adults

Special populations served: Mental retardation, physical disabilities, psychiatric disorders, hearing impairments and other: developmentally disabled (multiple)

Is there currently an HT program? Yes

When did the program begin? 1992

Number of clients per year: 18

Number of clients per group: 16

Indoor/Outdoor? Both, year-round

Equipment used: Adaptive tools, raised beds, containers and greenhouse

Activities: Herbs, crafts, indoor plants, annuals, perennials, landscape maintenance and landscape installation

Do participants sell horticultural products? No

Who is responsible for the horticultural therapy program? Horticultural Therapist

Who staffs the horticultural therapy program? Horticultural Therapist, aides and teacher
Number of staff: 3
Do you provide inservices/staff development? No
Are horticultural activities prescribed as a specific therapy? No
What are other means of enrolling in the program? Work incentive or workshop in controlled environment; process of elimination for assigning to various programs, mostly of sheltered workshops
What aspects of the program do you assess? Participant satisfaction, therapeutic progress, skill development, work quality index, attendance and knowledge of horticulture
How is your program funded? Government grants and fund raising events

* * *

Organization: Northshore Adult Day Health Center
9929-NE 180th
Bothell, WA 98011
USA
206-488-4821

Contact: Ms. Doris Coroch
Rehabilitation/Activity Specialist

Services provided: Case management; health screening; occupational therapy; physical therapy; speech therapy; recreational nurse; social work; caregivers support group. Recreational Therapy: Art, ceramics, horticulture, music, nature walks, special exercises, short outings, socialization, water therapy
Institution type: Rehabilitation center
Program type: Public, non-profit
Population served: Adults (ages 22-59) and older adults (ages 60 and over)
Special populations served: Physical disabilities
Is there currently an HT program? Yes. Weekly and monthly activities
When did the program begin? 1993
Number of clients per year: 10
Number of clients per group: 2-3
Indoor/Outdoor? Both, year-round
Equipment used: Raised beds and containers
Activities: Crafts, indoor plants, annuals and perennials
Do participants sell horticultural products? No
Who is responsible for the horticultural therapy program? Activity Therapist

Who staffs the horticultural therapy program? Activity Therapist and nurse, if needed
Number of staff: 2
Do you provide inservices/staff development? No
Are horticultural activities prescribed as a specific therapy? Yes
What are other means of enrolling in the program? Interest and skill level of participants
What aspects of the program do you assess? Participant satisfaction, therapeutic progress, skill development, attendance, and knowledge of horticulture
How is your program funded? Government grants and United Good Neighbors

*   *   *

Organization: Phelps-Clifton Springs, NY Central School District
2522 Lower Lake Road
Seneca Falls, NY 13148
USA
315-568-9736
(Fax) 607-255-9998

Contact: Mr. Vincent Lalli
Horticultural Therapy Intern

Services provided: Intergenerational Horticultural Therapy
Institution type: School
Program type: No response
Population served: Children, adults and older adults
Special populations served: Physical disabilities and psychiatric disorders
Is there currently an HT program? Yes. An intergenerational horticultural therapy flower bed planting project at the White Springs Senior Citizen's Manor, Geneva, NY, with the seniors and the local 4-H students
When did the program begin? 1995
Number of clients per year: 37
Number of clients per group: 18
Indoor/Outdoor? Both, year-round
Equipment used: Light carts, adaptive tools, raised beds, containers and greenhouse
Activities: Vegetable gardening, herbs, indoor plants, annuals, perennials and landscape maintenance
Do participants sell horticultural products? Yes

Who is responsible for the horticultural therapy program? Horticultural Therapy Intern
Who staffs the horticultural therapy program? Horticultural Therapist, nurse, volunteer, aides and Horticultural Therapy Intern
Number of staff: 5
Do you provide inservices/staff development? Yes
Are horticultural activities prescribed as a specific therapy? Yes
What are other means of enrolling in the program? Program enrollment is made up of Clifton Spa Apartment senior citizens, mental day care clients from Clifton Springs Hospital, learning disabled and intermediate school children
What aspects of the program do you assess? Participant satisfaction, therapeutic progress, skill development, attendance, knowledge of horticulture and attitude change
How is your program funded? Foundation grants, fund raising events, sale of products, private donations, school district

* * *

Organization: Providence Farm-St. Ann's Garden
1843 Tzouhalem Road RR5
Duncan, BC V9L 4T6
Canada
604-746-8982
(Fax) 604-746-8616

Contact: Ms. Christine Winter, HTR
Program Coordinator

Services provided: St. Ann's Garden comprises: allotment garden plots; public garden–safe for mentally ill and elderly; and garden club for mentally ill elderly
Institution type: Rehabilitation/garden center and arboretum
Program type: Public, non-profit
Population served: Older adults
Special populations served: Physical disabilities and psychiatric disorders
Is there currently an HT program? Yes. Weekly garden club for elderly still living at home, but have early signs of dementia
When did the program begin? 1994
Number of clients per year: 18
Number of clients per group: 6
Indoor/Outdoor? Both, year-round
Equipment used: Raised beds, containers and greenhouse

Activities: Vegetable gardening, fruit orchards, herbs, crafts, indoor plants, annuals, perennials, landscape maintenance and nature trails
Do participants sell horticultural products? No
Who is responsible for the horticultural therapy program? Horticultural Therapist
Who staffs the horticultural therapy program? Activity Therapist and volunteer
Number of staff: 2
Do you provide inservices/staff development? Yes
Are horticultural activities prescribed as a specific therapy? Yes
What are other means of enrolling in the program? Referral through outreach program at the local mental health centre
What aspects of the program do you assess? Participant satisfaction and attendance
How is your program funded? Government grants, donations/gifts and private donations

*   *   *

Organization: Rappahannock Adult Activities, Inc.
750 Kings Highway
Fredericksburg, VA 22405
USA
703-373-7643
(Fax) 703-373-2076

Contact: Ms. Becky Clark
Coordinator

Services provided: We grow a spring bedding crop, a fall mum crop and a poinsettia crop for sale. We offer our clients participation in all aspects of each crop. In the off-season we offer garden tours and walks, mainly activities in the community
Institution type: Day support program for adults with mental retardation
Program type: Public, for profit
Population served: Adults and older adults
Special populations served: Mental retardation and physical disabilities
Is there currently an HT program? Yes. We grow 3 major crops and involve clients in all aspects according to needs and abilities
When did the program begin? 1975
Number of clients per year: 10
Number of clients per group: 4

Indoor/Outdoor? Both, year-round
Equipment used: Raised beds, containers and greenhouse
Activities: Fruit orchards, crafts, annuals, perennials and nature trails
Do participants sell horticultural products? Yes
Who is responsible for the horticultural therapy program? Horticultural Therapist
Who staffs the horticultural therapy program? Horticultural therapist
Number of staff: 2
Do you provide inservices/staff development? No
Are horticultural activities prescribed as a specific therapy? Yes
What are other means of enrolling in the program? No response
What aspects of the program do you assess? Participant satisfaction and therapeutic progress
How is your program funded? Parent institution and sale of products

* * *

Organization: City of Southfield, Parks & Recreation, Senior Adult Center
24350 Civic Center Drive
Southfield, MI 48034
USA
810-354-9362
(Fax) 810-351-1300

Contact: Ms. Victoria L. Boase
Manager of Senior Services and Facilities

Services provided: Mary Thompson Senior Garden Program offers watered plots for the use of the city's seniors
Institution type: Senior citizen center
Program type: Public, non-profit
Population served: Adults (50+) and older adults (ages 60 and over)
Special populations served: No response
Is there currently an HT program? Yes
When did the program begin? 1980
Number of clients per year: 125
Number of clients per group: 1-2 per plot
Indoor/Outdoor? Seasonal, no response
Equipment used: Light carts
Activities: Vegetable gardening, herbs, nature trails and composting
Do participants sell horticultural products? Yes
Who is responsible for the horticultural therapy program? Master Gardeners

Who staffs the horticultural therapy program? Senior Adult Center
Number of staff: 3
Do you provide inservices/staff development? Yes
Are horticultural activities prescribed as a specific therapy? No
What are other means of enrolling in the program? Advertise with local media
What aspects of the program do you assess? Participant satisfaction, work quality index, and end of season Autumnfest with judging of produce by County Master Gardeners
How is your program funded? Municipal Parks District and Recreation Millage

*   *   *

Organization: Ruth Taylor Geriatric & Rehabilitation Institute
25 Bradhurst
Hawthorne, NY 10532
USA
914-285-1620

Contact: Ms. Maxine Jewel Kaplan, HTM
Horticultural Therapist

Services provided: Horticultural Therapy programs twice weekly serving dementia patients and physically disabled adult populations. Programming includes, teaching indoor gardening techniques and maintenance along with multi-sensory stimulation and reality orientation
Institution type: Nursing home
Program type: Public, non-profit
Population served: Adults (22-59) and older adults (60+)
Special populations served: Physical disabilities, psychiatric disorders and blindness
Is there currently an HT program? Yes. Teach indoor gardening techniques and maintenance along with multi-sensory stimulation and reality orientation
When did the program begin? 1981
Number of clients per year: 1500-2000
Number of clients per group: 6-12
Indoor/Outdoor? Both, year-round
Equipment used: Light carts, adaptive tools, raised beds and containers
Activities: Vegetable gardening, herbs, crafts, indoor plants and annuals
Do participants sell horticultural products? Yes

Who is responsible for the horticultural therapy program? Horticultural Therapist
Who staffs the horticultural therapy program? Horticultural Therapist
Number of staff: 1
Do you provide inservices/staff development? No
Are horticultural activities prescribed as a specific therapy? No
What are other means of enrolling in the program? Voluntary
What aspects of the program do you assess? Participant satisfaction, therapeutic progress, attendance, knowledge of horticulture and heightened interest and awareness
How is your program funded? Parent institution and county facility funded by county government

* * *

Organization: The Nathaniel Witherell
                          70 Parsonage Road
                          Greenwich, CT 06830
                          USA
                          203-869-4130

Contact: Ms. Swee-Lian Yi, HTR

Services provided: Nathaniel Witherell, situated in spacious homey surroundings, provides skilled nursing services for 202 beds. Year-round rehabilitative greenhouse program for various disabilities including MR and Alzheimer's patients. Greenhouse program was established in 1990. Activities include propagation and natural crafts
Institution type: Nursing home
Program type: Private, non-profit
Population served: Adults and older adults
Special populations served: Mental retardation, physical disabilities and Alzheimer's patients
Is there currently an HT program? Yes
When did the program begin? 1990
Number of clients per year: 1056
Number of clients per group: 6-7
Indoor/Outdoor? Both, year-round
Equipment used: Light carts, containers and greenhouse
Activities: Vegetable gardening, herbs, crafts, indoor plants and annuals
Do participants sell horticultural products? Yes

Who is responsible for the horticultural therapy program? Horticultural Therapist
Who staffs the horticultural therapy program? Volunteer
Number of staff: 5
Do you provide inservices/staff development? No
Are horticultural activities prescribed as a specific therapy? Yes
What are other means of enrolling in the program? At patient's or family's request
What aspects of the program do you assess? Participant satisfaction, therapeutic progress, skill development, attendance and knowledge of horticulture
How is your program funded? Parent institution, donations/gifts and private donations

*   *   *

Organization: TLC The Landscape Concern
            208 Serra Way
            Pomona, CA 91766
            USA
            909-627-4191

Contact: Mr. C. J. Blades
            HT Consultant

Services provided: Horticultural Therapy programs and services to a wide variety of dysfunctional people associated with both non-profit and for profit organizations
Institution type: Horticultural therapy services to institutions
Program type: Public, for profit
Population served: Adolescents (13-21), adults (22-59) and older adults (60+)
Special populations served: Mental retardation, physical disabilities, psychiatric disorders and Alzheimer's patients
Is there currently an HT program? Yes. I consult with various institutions to provide Horticultural Therapy programs
When did the program begin? 1989
Number of clients per year: 200
Number of clients per group: 8-15
Indoor/Outdoor? Both, year-round
Equipment used: Adaptive tools, raised beds and containers
Activities: Vegetable gardening, herbs, indoor plants, annuals and perennials
Do participants sell horticultural products? No

Who is responsible for the horticultural therapy program? Horticultural Therapist

Who staffs the horticultural therapy program? Horticultural Therapist

Number of staff: 0-6

Do you provide inservices/staff development? Yes

Are horticultural activities prescribed as a specific therapy? Yes

What are other means of enrolling in the program? No response

What aspects of the program do you assess? Participant satisfaction, rate of recovery, length of hospital stay, therapeutic process, attendance and general progress

How is your program funded? Parent institution and consulting fees

AHTA Survey of Programs for Older Adults—Selected Summary

Organization	Type of Institution	No. of Clients Served per Year	Person(s) Responsible for HT Program
American Association of Homes and Services for the Aging	No Response	No Response	No Response
Asbury Heights	Continuing care retirement community	50-100	Horticultural Therapist
Beverly Farm Foundation	Residential facility	345	Horticultural Therapist
Brandywine Nursing Home	Nursing home	No Response	Horticultural Therapist
CareWest	Nursing home	200	Recreational Therapist
Cheyenne Botanic Gardens	Botanic garden	80-100	Horticultural Therapist
Chicago Botanic Gardens Horticultural Therapy Services	Arboretum/garden center	450	Recreational Therapist
The Companion Gardener, Inc.	Nursing home	30-35	Horticultural Therapist
Crafts-Farrow State Hospital	Psychiatric institution	85	No Response
Ida Culver House Broadview	Nursing home	40	Horticultural Therapist
Eastern State Hospital	Psychiatric institution	220+	Horticultural Therapist
Forest Trace at Inverrary	Retirement center	780	Horticultural Therapist
Green Eacker's Vocational Training Program	Adult living home	8	Occupational Therapy Aide
Green Thumb, Inc.	No Response	No Response	No Response
Harmony House Health Care Center	Nursing home	100	Horticultural Therapist
HealthSouth RIOSA	Rehabilitation hospital	300	Recreational Therapist
Heather Farm Garden Center	Arboretum/garden center	500	Horticultural Therapist
Homewood Health Centre Hort. Therapy Dept.	Psychiatric institution	2600	Horticultural Therapist
La Vida Felicidad, Inc.	Other	17	Horticultural Therapist

Organization	Type of Institution	No. of Clients Served per Year	Person(s) Responsible for HT Program
Legacy Health System/ Legacy Portland Hospital	Rehabilitation hospital	300	Horticultural Therapist
The Lodge of Montgomery	Retirement center	50	Horticultural Therapist
Anita Lynne Home, Inc.	Domiciliary care facility w/ day program	30	Program Director
Memorial Hospital	Hospital	N/A	Horticultural Therapist
Mental Health Services, Inc.	Nursing home /comm. mental health center	7-10	Horticultural Therapist
Mercy Center for Health Care Services	Hospital	2600	Recreational Therapist
Meridian Perring Pkwy Member of the Genesis Health Venture	Nursing home	120-200	Horticultural Therapist
North Princeton Developmental Center	Sheltered workshop & vocational school	18	Horticultural Therapist
Northshore Adult Day Health Center	Rehabilitation center	10	Activity Therapist
Phelps-Clifton Springs NY Central School District	School	37	Horticultural Therapy Intern
Providence Farm St. Ann's Garden	Rehabilitation/garden center & arboretum	18	Horticultural Therapist
Rappahannock Adult Activities, Inc.	Day support program for adults w/MR	10	Horticultural Therapist
City of Southfield, Parks & Rec, Senior Adult Ctr.	Senior citizen center	125	Master Gardeners
Ruth Taylor Geriatric & Rehabilitation Institute	Nursing home	1500-2000	Horticultural Therapist
TLC The Landscape Concern	HT services to institutions	200	Horticultural Therapist
The Nathaniel Witherell	Nursing home	1056	Horticultural Therapist
Dr. Yeager Health Center	Nursing home	50	Occupational Therapist

Bibliography

Anderson, H. (1992, June). Gardeners lend a hand. *New Zealand Gardener, 48(6)*, 24.

An ingenious retirement garden. (1992, June). *New Zealand Gardener, 48(6)*, 34-37.

Atkin, E. E. (1982). Beyond the garden salad: A therapeutic garden and food awareness program. *National Council for Therapy and Rehabilitation Through Horticulture, 10th Annual Conference.*

Breed, J. (1986, Spring). The flowering of horticulture at Amsterdam House. *Journal of Gerontological Social Work, 9(3)*, 95-97.

Browne, C. A. (1991). The role of nature for the promotion of well-being of the elderly. In D. Relf (Ed.), *The Role of Horticulture in Human Well-Being and Social Development: A National Symposium.* Portland, OR: Timber Press.

Bryant, W. (1991, May). Creative group work with confused elderly people: A development of sensory integration therapy. *British Journal of Occupational Therapy, 54(5)*, 187-192.

Bubel, N. (1990, September/October). A therapy garden. *Country Journal, 17(5)*, 74-77.

Burgess, C. W. (1990). Horticulture and its application to the institutionalized elderly. *Activities, Adaptation & Aging, 14(3)*, 51-61.

Carstens, D. Y. (1985). *Site planning and design for the elderly: Issues, guidelines, and alternatives.* New York, NY: Van Nostrand Reinhold.

Cattell, M. G. (1992). *Gardens and social order in a Philadelphia neighborhood.* Paper presented at the 1993 annual meeting of the Society for Cross-Cultural Research, Washington, DC.

Cox, R. (1986, November). Alverno Green Thumb Club grows strong community ties. *Provider, 12(11)*, 68-71.

Dowling, J. R. (1995). *Keeping busy: A handbook of activities for persons with dementia* (Chapter 10, 143-151). Baltimore, MD: The Johns Hopkins University Press.

Epstein, S. G. & Greenberger, D. S. (1990). Nurturing plants, children, and older individuals: Intergenerational horticultural therapy. *Journal of Therapeutic Horticulture, 5*, 16-19.

Fliegel, J. C. (1988). *Some influences of horticultural and social activities on blood pressure of elderly people.* Unpublished Master's Thesis, Kansas State University, Manhattan, KS.

Gallagher, M. J. (1984). *Measuring arthritic hand skill performance during horticultural activities.* Unpublished Master's Thesis, Kansas State University, Manhattan, KS.

Gassoway, B. M. (1990). Conducting horticultural therapy research: A methodological essay. *Journal of Therapeutic Horticulture, 5*, 20-40.

Giancone, J. (1979, March). Gardening and the blind older adult. *HortTherapy, 1*, 19-39.

Gibson, H. E. (1990, November/December). Taking the pain out of gardening:

Old age and physical disabilities don't have to force people to give up a favorite hobby like gardening. *Flower & Garden Magazine, 34,* 78.

Gobster, P.H. (1991). Trends in urban forest recreation: Trail use patterns and perceptions of older adults. In *Proceedings of the National Outdoor Recreation Trends Symposium III* (pp. 286-295). Indianapolis, IN.

Goodban, A. & Goodban, D. (1990, November). Horticultural therapy: A growing concern (part 2). *British Journal of Occupational Therapy, 53(11),* 468-70.

Greishaw, S. (1980). My, these are beautiful flowers. *American Journal of Nursing, 80(10),* 1782-1783.

Hagedorn, R. (1991, October). Horticulture as a prescriptive tool for behavioral change. *Professional Horticulture, 5(3),* 129-133.

Haley, E. (1987, June). Gardening at Blue Ridge Center promotes growth in many ways. *Provider, 13(6),* 44-45.

Hamilton, L., Nichols, P. J. R., & White, A.S. (1970). Gardening for the disabled and elderly. *Royal Horticulture Society Journal, 95,* 358-369.

Hefley, P. D. (1972). *An investigation of horticulture as a technique for the rehabilitation of the older institutionalized mentally retarded individuals.* Unpublished Master's Thesis, University of Maryland, College Park, MD.

Hill, C. O. (1980). *Resident acceptance of outdoor gardening in two geriatric institutions.* Unpublished Master's Thesis, Virginia Polytechnic Institute and State University, Blacksburg, VA.

Hill, C. O., & Relf, P. D. (1983). Gardening as an outdoor activity in geriatric institutions. *Activities, Adaptation & Aging, 3(1),* 47-54.

Hilliker, F. (1970). Patients grow active as they grow plants. *Modern Nursing Home, 25,* 48-49.

Hogan, D. (1981). Designing a model nursing home garden. *HortTherapy, 1(2),* 44-48.

Honey, T. E. (1991, October). The many faces of horticultural therapy. *American Horticulturist,* 19-23.

Horne, D. C. (1974). *An evaluation of the effectiveness of horticultural therapy on the life satisfaction level of aged persons confined to a rest care facility.* Unpublished Master's Thesis, Clemson University, Clemson, SC.

Houseman, D. (1986). Developing links between horticultural therapy and aging. *Journal of Therapeutic Horticulture, 1,* 9-14.

Houseman, D. (1990). *The role of horticulture in an aging population.* Presentation conducted at a meeting of the Canadian Horticultural Therapy Association.

Howard, D. (1986, December). Raised beds, raised spirits. *National Gardening, 9(12),* 48-49.

Hunter, A. B. (1983). *Evaluation of a horticultural therapy program at Ithacare Center.* Class Project, Ithaca, NY: Cornell University.

Inman, M. & Duffus, J. (1984-85). Adaptations to dwellings and interiors by independent older adults following relocation. *Journal of Housing for the Elderly, 2(4),* 51-61.

Johnson, P. H. (1987, May). Gardening saved his life. *Rodale's Organic Gardening, 34,* 60-64.

Killeffer, E. H. P., Bennett, R., & Gruen, G. (1985). *Handbook of Innovative Programs for the Impaired Elderly.* New York: The Haworth Press, Inc.

Langer, E. J. & Rodin, J. (1976). The effects of choice and enhanced personal responsibility for the aged: A field experiment in an institutional setting. *Journal of Personality and Social Psychology, 34(2),* 191-198.

Lewis, J. F. & Mattson, R. H. (1988). Gardening may reduce blood pressure of elderly people: Activity suggestions and models for intervention. *Journal of Therapeutic Horticulture, 3,* 25-38.

Long, J. (1992, February/March). Pencil Gardens. *The Herb Companion, 4(3),* 12.

Lyons, E. (1983, July). Demographic correlates of landscape preference. *Environment and Behavior, 15(4),* 487-511.

Mattson, R. H. & Hilbert, R. T. (1976). Psychological, social, physical and educational effects of horticultural therapy for geriatrics. *HortScience, 11,* 328.

McAndrew, W. P. (1980). *An analysis of horticultural therapy activities in licensed nursing homes.* Unpublished Master's Thesis, Kansas State University, Manhattan, KS.

Meadowcroft, J. (1992, March). Gardening in a retirement village. *New Zealand Gardening, 48(3),* 12-14.

Mooney, P. & Nicell, P. Lenore. (1992, Summer). The importance of exterior enviroment for Alzheimer Residents: Effective care and Risk management. *Healthcare Management Forum,* 23-29.

Moore, B. (1989). *Growing with Gardening: A twelve-month guide for therapy, recreation, and education.* Chapel Hill, NC: University of North Carolina Press.

National Library Service for the Blind and Physically Handicapped. (1981, September). *Gardening for handicapped and elderly persons: Bibliography no. 81-1.* Washington, DC: Gibson, M.

Pitt, E. J. (1984). *Factors which affect the preferences of the elderly for hand pruners.* Unpublished Master's Thesis, Virginia Polytechnic Institute and State University, Blacksburg, VA.

Pitt-Nairn, E. J., Relf, P. D., & McDaniel, A. R. (1992). Analysis of factors which can affect the preferences of older individuals for hand pruners. *Physical and Occupational Therapy in Geriatrics, 10,* 4.

Please, P. (1990). *Able to garden: A practical guide for disabled and elderly gardeners.* London: B. T. Batsford, Ltd.

Powell, L., Flece, D., Jenkins, J., & Lunt, B. (1979). Increasing engagement in a home for the elderly by providing an indoor gardening activity. *Behavior Research and Therapy, 17(2),* 127-135.

Relf (Hefley), P. D. (1972). *An investigation of horticulture as a technique for the rehabilitation of the older institutionalized mentally retarded individual.* Unpublished Master's Thesis, University of Maryland, College Park, MD.

Relf, P.D. (1978, September). Horticulture as a recreational activity. *American Health Care Association Journal, 14(5),* 68-70.

Relf, P. D. (1994). *Gardening in raised beds and containers.* Blacksburg, VA: Virginia Cooperative Extension Service.

Riordan, R. J. & Williams, C. S. (1988). Gardening therapeutics for the elderly. *Activities, Adaptation & Aging, 12(1-2),* 103-111.

Robb, S. S., Boyd, M., & Pristash, C. L. (1980). A wind bottle, plant, and puppy: Catalysts for social behavior. *Journal of Gerontology Nursing, 6(12),* 721-728.

Rodin, J. & Langer, E. J. (1977). Long term effects of control-relevant intervention with the institutionalized aged. *Journal of Personality and Social Psychology, 35(12),* 897-902.

Rothert, E. A. & Danbert, J. R. (1981). *Horticultural therapy for nursing homes, senior centers, retirement living.* Glencoe, IL: Chicago Horticultural Society.

Roweton, W. E. (1981). Older adults, horticulture, and institutional life: Afterthoughts from a volunteer. *Great Plains Journal of Horticulture Therapy, 1(3).*

Schultz, W. (1987, March). Age is no barrier. *National Gardening.*

Smith, K. (1990). Techniques in topiary for special populations. *Proceedings of the American Horticultural Therapy Association, 18th Annual Conference.*

Some tips on tools for elderly and handicapped gardeners. (1984). *Mother Earth News,* 70-73.

Somers, M. (1982, August). Seasons of the mind: Plant life and personal growth among the aged. *Proceedings of the National Council for Therapy and Rehabilitation through Horticulture, 19th Annual Conference.*

South Carolina Agriculture Experiment Station. (1976). *Indoor horticultural activities for nursing homes* (Publication 17). Clemson University: Fox, S.

Stoneham, J.A. & Thoday, P.R. (1944). *Landscape design for elderly and disabled people.* Woodbridge: Antique Collector's Club.

Thoday, P. R. & Stoneham, J. A. (1989). Amenity horticulture and its contribution to the quality of life. *Professional Horticulture, (3),* 5-7.

Tinsley, H. E. A., Teaff, J. D., Colbs, S. L., & Kaufman, N. (1985). A system of classifying leisure activities in terms of the psychological benefits of participation reported by older persons. *Journal of Gerontology, 40(2),* 172-178.

Tips on coping with arthritis. (1990, April). *Horticulture, 68(4),* 18.

Train, R. (1976). *The effect of horticultural therapy in maintaining life satisfaction of geriatrics.* Unpublished Master's Thesis, Kansas State University, Manhattan, KS.

Tyson, M. M. (1987). Memories of Grandma's backyard. *Journal of Therapeutic Horticulture, 2,* 29-35.

USDA Forest Service, North Central Forest Experiment Station, Urban Forestry Unit (1990). *The benefits of nearby nature for elderly apartment residents.* (Urban Forestry Unit Cooperative Agreement 23-87-03). Talbot, J. F. & Kaplan, R.

Van der Hoeven, G. (1989, November). Thoughts on designing landscapes for unique and elderly people. In R. H. Mattson (Ed.), *Proceedings of Where the Rainbow Begins, Therapeutic Horticulture Short Course #8.*

Weatherly, L. & Weatherly, K. (1990, September). Containerized vegetable gardening for homebound patients. *Caring, 9(9),* 52-54.

White, A. S. & Lake, C. (1973). Gardening for the disabled. *Nursing Times, 69(21)*, 678-680.

Whittier, D. (1979, April). Horticultural activities for physical disabilities of the elderly. *National Council for Therapy and Rehabilitation Through Horticulture, 6*, 3-5.

Willcox, R. T. & Mattson, R. H. (1979). Horticultural therapy maintains life-satisfaction of geriatrics. *Great Plains Journal of Horticultural Therapy, 1(1)*.

Zube, E. H., Pitt, D. G., & Evans, G. W. (1983). A lifespan developmental study of landscape assessment. *Journal of Environmental Psychology, (3)*, 115-128.

Index

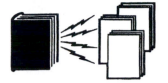

Haworth
DOCUMENT DELIVERY
SERVICE

This valuable service provides a single-article order form for any article from a Haworth journal.

- *Time Saving:* No running around from library to library to find a specific article.
- *Cost Effective:* All costs are kept down to a minimum.
- *Fast Delivery:* Choose from several options, including same-day FAX.
- *No Copyright Hassles:* You will be supplied by the original publisher.
- *Easy Payment:* Choose from several easy payment methods.

Open Accounts Welcome for ...
- Library Interlibrary Loan Departments
- Library Network/Consortia Wishing to Provide Single-Article Services
- Indexing/Abstracting Services with Single Article Provision Services
- Document Provision Brokers and Freelance Information Service Providers

---

MAIL or *FAX* THIS ENTIRE ORDER FORM TO:

Haworth Document Delivery Service
The Haworth Press, Inc.
10 Alice Street
Binghamton, NY 13904-1580

or **FAX:** 1-800-895-0582
or **CALL:** 1-800-342-9678
9am-5pm EST

PLEASE SEND ME PHOTOCOPIES OF THE FOLLOWING SINGLE ARTICLES:

1) Journal Title: _____

    Vol/Issue/Year:_____Starting & Ending Pages:_____

Article Title:_____

_____

2) Journal Title: _____

    Vol/Issue/Year:_____Starting & Ending Pages:_____

Article Title:_____

_____

3) Journal Title: _____

    Vol/Issue/Year:_____Starting & Ending Pages:_____

Article Title:_____

_____

4) Journal Title: _____

    Vol/Issue/Year:_____Starting & Ending Pages:_____

Article Title:_____

_____

(See other side for Costs and Payment Information)

COSTS: Please figure your cost to order quality copies of an article.

1. Set-up charge per article: $8.00
   ($8.00 × number of separate articles) _____

2. Photocopying charge for each article:

   1-10 pages: $1.00 _____

   11-19 pages: $3.00 _____

   20-29 pages: $5.00 _____

   30+ pages: $2.00/10 pages _____

3. Flexicover (optional): $2.00/article _____

4. Postage & Handling: US: $1.00 for the first article/
   $.50 each additional article _____

   Federal Express: $25.00 _____

   Outside US: $2.00 for first article/
   $.50 each additional article _____

5. Same-day FAX service: $.35 per page _____

   GRAND TOTAL: _____

METHOD OF PAYMENT: (please check one)

❑ Check enclosed   ❑ Please ship and bill. PO # _____
(sorry we can ship and bill to bookstores only! All others must pre-pay)

❑ Charge to my credit card: ❑ Visa; ❑ MasterCard; ❑ Discover;
❑ American Express;

Account Number:_____ Expiration date:_____

Signature: ✗_____

Name: _____ Institution: _____

Address: _____

_____

City: _____ State:_____ Zip:_____

Phone Number: _____ FAX Number: _____

MAIL or *FAX* THIS ENTIRE ORDER FORM TO:

Haworth Document Delivery Service
The Haworth Press, Inc.
10 Alice Street
Binghamton, NY 13904-1580

or FAX: 1-800-895-0582
or CALL: 1-800-342-9678
9am-5pm EST)